BIKING to BLISSVILLE

BIKING to BLISSVILLE

A Cycling Guide
to the Maritimes and the Magdalen Islands

Kent Thompson

GOOSE LANE

Published with the assistance of the Canada Council, Communications Canada and the New Brunswick Department of Municipalities, Culture and Housing, 1993.

Cover photograph by Brian Atkinson
Back cover photograph by Michaele Thompson
Book design by Brenda Steeves and Julie Scriver
Maps by Sean Duffey
Printed in Canada by Gagné Printing.
10 9 8 7 6 5 4 3 2

Canadian Cataloguing in Publication Data

Thompson, Kent, 1936 —

Biking to Blissville

Includes bibliographical references and index.
ISBN 0-86492-154-3

1. Bicycle touring — Maritime Provinces — Guidebooks.   2. Bicycle touring — Quebec (Province) — Îles-de-la-Madeleine — Guidebooks.   3. Maritime Provinces — Guidebooks.   4. Îles-de-la-Madeleine (Quebec) — Guidebooks. I. Title.

GV1046.C3T46 1993   796.6'4'09715   C93-098595-8

Goose Lane Editions
469 King Street
Fredericton, New Brunswick
Canada E3B 1E5

Contents

Acknowledgements

Many people assisted in many different ways in the creation of this book, but special acknowledgement and thanks should go to the novelist and poet Elisabeth Harvor, who grew up on the Kingston Peninsula of New Brunswick and suggested something very like the title of this book; to Peter Williams of Sussex, New Brunswick, who researched rides (some of which have been used, in whole or in part, for this book) for Velo New Brunswick and the New Brunswick Department of Economic Development and Tourism; to Greg West, of the New Brunswick Department of Economic Development and Tourism, for his maps and advice, and experience of cycling in New Brunswick; to Francine Godin, of the New Brunswick Department of Tourism, Recreation, and Heritage, for her good offices, efficiency and helpful, cheerful energy; to Sean Duffey for his devotion to providing the guide with good maps; to Kevin of the Dalvay Inn By The Sea, Prince Edward Island, for providing a history of that hotel; to young Jonathan Campbell of Port Hood, Nova Scotia, who provided companionship and wanted to be in the book and now is; to Lane MacIntosh and Bill Gould of Fredericton, New Brunswick, who were grand guides and companions on several of the rides; to Art and Beth Tracy for Maineland advice; to Mike at Ski-Wolf for making my bicycle zing sweet songs; to Laurel Boone, for editing my prose with a close eye and excellent taste (and who is not responsible for any of the wilder flights of fancy or unorthodox syntax to be found in these pages); and to my wife, Michaele, who played the demanding role of Ms. Luxe to perfection.

In addition, I would like to thank the following publishers for granting me permission to quote from the books in their collections: to Farrar Straus Giroux for *The Collected Prose of Elizabeth Bishop* © 1984; to HarperCollins Publishers for *Immortality* by Milan Kundera (translated by Peter Kussi) © 1992; to Pantheon Books for *About Looking* by John Berger © 1980; and to Macmillan Canada for *The Moons of Jupiter* by Alice Munro © 1979.

KT

An Introduction

We think we know who you are. We think you have a couple of bicycles hanging off the back of your car. We think you're probably over thirty, and on holiday with a dear companion. (How's that for tact?) We think you are a *recreational rider*.

And the intention of this book is to offer the recreational rider some guidance to something a little special — where to ride, where to stay — in the Maritime provinces.

The Maritime provinces of Canada — for strangers who might not know — are New Brunswick, Nova Scotia and Prince Edward Island. We've added the Magdalen Islands (Îles de la Madeleine) just for fun, even though they're part of Québec.

As you will soon discover, it is a bit misleading to lump the three provinces together under one term, as if they were all alike. You will find them quite distinct. Prince Edward Island, for example, is almost entirely pastoral: it is full of farms, most of them quite tidy, some of them beautiful. You will cycle through well-kept fields, and, at the right time of year, you'll find the roadsides decorated with iris and lupin.

Nova Scotia, on the other hand, has different areas with distinct personalities. Lunenburg is a famous old shipbuilding centre and fishing port; the Annapolis Valley has been glorified with orchards and rich farmland since the seventeenth century; and the hills above the sea near Mabou, in Cape Breton Island, Nova Scotia, offer the most beautiful ride in the world. I think so, anyway.

New Brunswick seems at first glance to be nothing but trees, interrupted by the broad and beautiful St. John River and characterized by famous sport-fishing streams like the Miramichi. When you think about the North Woods you can think about New Brunswick. The Krieghoff paintings are more accurate than you might suppose. But there are dairy centres like Sussex and the old and elegant town of St. Andrews, as well — and the French personality of the Acadian peninsula, where at Lamèque you will find tall churches, peat fields and baroque music.

It's obvious but true: each place is different from every other place. Even within a single ride you will probably find little surprises, little differences in history and landscape or seascape which you can tuck into your memory to tell your friends back home, or your grandchildren. I have tried to find rides in different parts of each province

— so that wherever you find yourself in the Maritimes, you can open this book and find a half-day's bicycle exercise not too far away.

Incidentally, all of the provinces publish large, thick, and excellent travel guides which are available free at every information bureau in each province. They are all excellent, giving you history of the area, campground locations, and accommodations available — and the one for the Magdalen Islands is outstanding. I recommend them highly.

Riding around in circles

Virtually every ride suggested in this book is a loop. You return to the place you started. We think you will probably drive to one of the places suggested in **Where to Stay**, and cycle out from there and return there.

The loops are of various lengths, but most of them are between 30 and 50 km (19 and 31 mi). The cycling time is usually between 1 and 3 hrs. Most of the suggested routes are designated Moderate; some few are Easy; one or two are Difficult. We assume that you are riding for exercise and fun and are not especially interested in amassing amazing numbers. We assume you are not in training for any marathon except life.

The suggested routes have been selected for their interest — usually scenic — and their safety. I have put wheels to all of the roads I suggest, and if for one reason or another I had to drive part of a loop in a vehicle, I have told you exactly where.

The book is arranged west to east, left to right, because that's how we usually read. The rides are arranged in something like a big circle around New Brunswick, from the western tip of Prince Edward Island to the eastern tip, and in a zigzag across Nova Scotia. The arrangements have much to do with topography and available roads, but I have done my best to find rides all over each province. In the Magdalen Islands I take you in tight little circles, like this: o o o.

Many other routes were driven — and rejected for this book — or ridden on a bike — and rejected for this book. When this book was being created I found myself time and again muttering under my breath that I wished I had a book (like this one) to guide me, because I soon discovered that maps are wonderful — but never a sufficient guide to the road or locality. And I soon had a Rule for myself: never cycle a road that hasn't been driven first. It was a good rule. Once I found myself in my old blue van heaving through a mud slough which, on the map, seemed to be a nice little country road. It was an Adventure, but not exactly fun. I spent a long time in the truck wash with that old van. Or, more than once, I found myself cycling a road which I decided was too dangerous to recommend to anyone who wanted to ride for fun. But it looked just fine on the map.

What do the terms Easy, Moderate and Difficult mean? An Easy ride will be flat and probably no more than 30 km (19 mi). You may ride the entire route using your largest chainwheel. A Difficult ride will often have at least a couple of mean hills requiring granny-gears. (A granny-gear is one which utilizes your smallest chainwheel. The *chainwheel* is the sprocket driven directly by your foot. The little sprockets on your rear hub which accept the chain are now usually called *freewheels*. At your slowest speed on the steepest hill you are using your smallest chainwheel and your largest freewheel. That's your bottom granny-gear. When you get down into your granny-gears you're puffing — and you are not going very fast — hence "granny-gear." Sorry, granny.)

A Moderate ride might have one or two short hills. You will use your granny-gears once or twice.

Where to Stay

Each ride or loop is usually fastened (as it were) to a campground and an interesting bed-and-breakfast or country inn. You can therefore decide on a holiday or weekend excursion in mother nature's bosom, or combine your refreshing exercise with the coddling and ambience of a unique bed and breakfast or country inn. (The two terms are not synonymous: the country inn does not always provide a breakfast in the price of the room, but does frequently have a dining room for lunches and evening meals. Moreover, the term *inn* is used a little differently in each province.)

What I am offering you, therefore, is the opportunity to create your own cycling holiday. You can cycle on a budget and camp — or you can imitate the international cycling tours (which produce such lovely glossy brochures) and stay in some of the same inns — or you can mix 'n' match. Some of the hostelries suggested are very elegant indeed, with rates to match; others are more modest but charming and unique — and selected not least of all because they are especially hospitable to cyclists — and a few of them are wonderful bargains. If some of these are given stars by their provincial evaluating agency, I note the award — but stars are usually awarded for the extensive facilities, not charm.

Most of these (not all) have been checked out by the team of Joe Spartan (that's me) and Ms. Luxe, who is the woman with whom I live. She does love the elegant life and it suits her. She is quite at home in a drawing room, and can pronounce with assurance on gourmet cuisine. She is one of the very few people I know who reads cookbooks the way other people read thrillers. But, as the result of a deprived childhood, she cannot ride a bicycle. Oh, the pity of it!

I, on the other hand, will happily doss down in the back of the old blue van and hop out the next morning unshaven and onto my bike, eager for the road. You will probably notice that I am by turns cheerful, grumpy, and ecstatic. The road is a romance for me, and if you don't happen to share my attitude, tough. I am also right arty and I'll be damned if I'll apologize for that, either.

The campgrounds, by the way, differ considerably in the four provinces. In New Brunswick the provincial parks and campgrounds, built by the government to similar standards and plans, are now frequently operated privately or by the local community or a service club. They will have electricity, water handy, and the hot showers and flush toilets which make camping less primitive than otherwise. The private campgrounds in New Brunswick usually attempt to meet the standard set by the provincial campgrounds.

A similar situation exists in Prince Edward Island, where the provincial campgrounds are still operated by the government. The provincial campgrounds are uniformly excellent and especially hospitable to cyclists. When you meet other cyclists on the road, they talk warmly about Prince Edward Island provincial campgrounds. The situation is markedly different in Nova Scotia. The next time somebody tells you, "Private enterprise can do anything better than the government," tell them about the Nova Scotia campgrounds. With a couple of exceptions, private campgrounds in Nova Scotia are (I'm searching for the polite word here, and failing) abominable.

Why? Because the government offers them no competition. You will in fact see many, many Nova Scotia provincial campgrounds, and, when you wheel in, you are delighted: all of them are nicely laid out, shaded, groomed, clean — and virtually empty. In more than one case, at the height of the season, I found a Nova Scotia provincial campground utterly deserted. Not a single person there.The reason is simple. All but three Nova Scotia provincial parks have only unserviced sites, and offer only pit toilets — and no hot water, no showers, no electricity. Those amenities are left to private enterprise. And private enterprise, with a captive market, is pretty casual about standards, and, in my experience anyway, not interested in tenters.

The Magdalen Islands/Îles de la Madeleine are part of the province of Québec, and have only private campgrounds. As is common in Québec, the campgrounds are of two sorts: party campgrounds and nature campgrounds. The former usually have a nightclub attached; the latter do not. I prefer the latter. But you will find that Québecers are keen campers and will obtain and display the most colourful and interesting tents imaginable. A good Québec campground looks like flowers in the forest — or a medieval festival.

Equipment

What is absolutely essential?

Well, a bicycle, of course — although you'll find a surprising number of country inns and bed and breakfasts where bicycles are provided free or for rent, and a few campgrounds where rental bicycles are available. You should have your own helmet and some comfortable clothes.

The bike you use will probably be a so-called mountain bike — which is to say, a bike with fat tires — because mountain bikes have captured the bicycle market, and with good reason. The mountain bicycle is very stable (because of its fat tires and flat handlebars) and very forgiving. You can hit a pothole in a city street or a log on a country road and bounce happily onward. (There is a reason why the mad bicycle couriers of large cities use mountain bikes.) And if a paved road becomes uncomfortably clogged with motor vehicles, you can often take to the gravelled shoulder and cycle merrily on.

The hybrid will offer you some of the same advantages. The hybrid is in fact simply a mountain bike with narrower tires. The narrower tire gives you more speed on pavement — on good pavement, if you can find good pavement. And a hybrid will let you ride most dirt and/or gravel roads. Like the mountain bike, the hybrid has the flat handlebars which give you lateral stability, and, as with the mountain bike, you are up comparatively high and can see what's coming.

The ten-speed bike — or road bike — is much less popular now than it was only a decade ago — and the change in bicycles is part of the impetus behind this book. Most of the older guides to cycling were written with the ten-speed bike in mind, and the ten-speed bike is restricted to paved roads. It is, moreover, comparatively vulnerable. When you have a ten-speed bike you plan to repair your tires often, and I have done so. But with the mountain bike I used for this book I had only one flat tire — and that occurred when I ran over a stray thumb-tack inexplicably in the middle of nowhere.

But should you acquire a top-quality bicycle?

Not necessarily. If you hang around bicycle shops (cyclists hang around bike shops the way alcoholics hang around bars), you will hear the so-called "department store bike" much mocked, but — in my opinion — undeservedly. I rode many of these routes with a department store bike and it did very well by me. The chief differences between a comparatively cheap bicycle and an expensive bicycle are two: the department store bicycle will be a good deal heavier than the expensive bike (and therefore you have to peddle that weight as well as your own), and the gears and brakes on the department store bike will demand more attention and adjustment. You will find, in fact, that the department store bike will almost always have a guarantee on its frame, and its frame will be strong, sturdy and heavy. But the trouble will come with the gearing and braking; the cheaper alloys don't hold their adjustments.

The candid truth is, however, that I am not an equipment freak — which causes me some uneasy moments in the bike shops. In bike shops you are expected to discourse easily on the merits of your bicycle and its gears and brakes, and you are judged on your knowledge. Since I have a hard time remembering the stuff which makes my bike perform so admirably, I am considering taping a cheat-sheet to my wrist for use in bike shops — just as a new quarterback has to tape a list of plays on his wrist before a football game. But you need a helmet. This is worth repeating: you need a helmet. You will (still) hear some people say you don't, but there are easy responses to that idle notion. Here's one: The Only People Who Should Not Wear Helmets are Those Who Have Nothing Worth Protecting. Consider that. Consider that all the international bicycle tours require helmets. There's a reason for that, you know. Or try this: Fetch a fresh egg from the refrigerator. Hold it eight inches above a bowl. Drop the egg into the bowl. Consider your head. Look at the brains spilled out into the bowl. Scramble the eggs. Consider your head. Don't be a fool.

For all that, it is difficult to put a helmet on for the first time if you have grown up without wearing one. A bicycle is usually one of a kid's first toys, and as people grow up they continue to think of it as a toy rather than as a means of transportation or as sporting equipment for venturesome exercise. But after you have worn a helmet once, you'll find it feels comfy and right — and fashionable, too. Right snazzy. Demonstrates the active life. Takes years off you.

If there is one addition to basic equipment which you want to consider, it might be hiking boots. That's right: hiking boots — boots with a stiff sole. Hiking boots are infinitely better than sneakers for cycling, and the reason is easy to demonstrate. When you push down on a pedal you are pushing the weight of the bike against your foot. If your foot has to take all that weight on a sneaker, your foot gets tired. Hiking boots are a great investment.

I learned this first from my son, who has been my mentor in a biking career to which I returned after a hiatus of many years. He is one of those fellows who uses a mountain bike to climb trees, and whose idea of a really good time is to cycle down a mountain in a dry creek bed — at night. But it was he who saved my life when I returned to cycling with some good advice which I here pass on to you: 1) Remember that brakes do not work as well in the rain as in dry conditions and calculate accordingly; and 2) Remember to brake *all the way down a steep hill*; don't wait until you are hurtling toward the bottom to apply your brakes. I had not known the one and had forgotten the other.

He also recommended toe-clips, so I dutifully acquired toe-clips — and for the first month couldn't understand their virtues. Then I realized that instead of pedalling my bike, I was wearing it, and became a believer. But I am not yet ready for the latest thing: cleat-pedals which require special shoes. I'm sticking with the multi-purpose hiking boots.

After you have the helmet and the hiking boots you can consider the cycling shorts. Yeah, they look great. Yeah, you walk into the donut shop with your water bottle in hand and you get looks which are not considering the water bottle.

Even better, when you've been cycling for a while, you've got something worth looking at.

What you should carry with you on the road
You should carry a simple repair kit and a spare tube and a pump. One of you should know how to change a tire. (Don't forget the tire irons.) You probably won't need the tools or the tube (especially if you're riding a mountain bike), but it feels comfortable to be well-equipped for an emergency. You should carry at least one full water bottle per person — and something to eat. I carry muffins and apples. You should also have fly-dope for our frequently savage blackflies and sunblock for the days which are almost too glorious to endure.

Maps
The real reason you have purchased this book is for the maps. Maps tell you at a glance where you are (assurance is wonderful) and where you ought go next. "If only life had a map!" you say.

More to the point, the maps should offer you visible suggestions for a good holiday or a rewarding weekend.

In addition, however, all of the routes indicated on the maps are supported by printed instructions. We want you to feel comfy. Distance are approximate, within a kilometre or half a mile. Is *any* odometer absolutely trustworthy?

You will find all manner of surfaces on the roads of the Maritime provinces. You will find asphalt, patched asphalt, chipseal (fine gravel and tar trying to be asphalt), gravel (large gravel, small gravel) and dirt. Sometimes mud. I try to guide you away from mud.

Commentary

One of the joys of a book with maps and descriptions is that you can use the commentary or not, as you choose. For each ride I have offered some of my own reactions, responses, thoughts or notions. You can skip these if you like; you won't get lost if you do. My feelings won't be hurt; I won't know.

But you might enjoy the commentaries, too. I tried always to find a somewhat different means of looking at a locality: different from the usual tourist guides, perhaps. I am a somewhat different fellow, perhaps. Clearly I am fond of literature and art. (Fond? That ain't the half of it. *Life without Art is not worth living!*) Moreover, for me cycling is an aesthetic quest. I take it as axiomatic that Beauty cannot be found without effort. And you will notice that I am fond of quoting bits and pieces of things from here and there. Like this reflective comment from Milan Kundera's *Immortality*. You can substitute the word *cycle* for *walk*, if you like. I think that's fair, don't you?

Road: a strip of ground over which one walks. A highway differs from a road not only because it is solely intended for vehicles, but also because it is merely a line that connects one point with another. A highway has no meaning in itself; its meaning derives entirely from the two points that it connects. A road is a tribute to space. Every stretch of road has meaning in itself and invites us to stop. A highway is the triumphant devaluation of space, which thanks to it has been reduced to a mere obstacle to movement and a waste of time.

That's worth considering, isn't? Highways and roads are different, and "a road is a tribute to space."

Yep. Enjoy the roads.

Kent Thompson
Fredericton, New Brunswick
1993

NEW BRUNSWICK

1. Grand Manan
2. St. Andrews
3. Blissville
4. Harvey Lake
5. Mactaquac Country
6. St. John River

7. Sussex Valley
8. Boiestown, Ludlow and Doaktown
9. Campbellton
10. Maisonnette and Caraquet
11. Lamèque
12. Kouchibouguac

GRAND MANAN

Ride One
DISTANCE: 26 km (16 mi)
TIME: 1 hr 30 min
DIFFICULTY: Moderate
OTHER FACTORS: Granny-gear hills and rough gravel road near Southwest Light.

Ride Two
DISTANCE: 45 km (28 mi) including Whistle Road diversion 18 km (11 mi) from campground to Swallow Tail Lighthouse; 36 km (22 mi) return. 9 km (5.5 mi) diversion to Whistle Lighthouse and back.
TIME: 3 hrs
DIFFICULTY: Easy to Moderate

Ride Three
DISTANCE: 30 km (19 mi)
TIME: 2 hrs
DIFFICULTY: Hard
OTHER FACTORS: Long, steep gravel road to Dark Harbour.

Ride Four
DISTANCE: 20 km (12 mi)
TIME: 1 hr + 25 minute ferry
DIFFICULTY: Easy

Queen of the Fundy Isles

You leave for the island of Grand Manan from the little New Brunswick fishing port of Blacks Harbour. Blacks Harbour is the centre of the sardine industry in New Brunswick. You can smell it some distance away, and you can buy tins of sardines (if that's your fancy) at the factory outlet store (if you like factory outlet stores) in Blacks Harbour. And you might want to prepare yourself to wait a couple of hours for the ferry. A wait is usual in the summertime. You can read this book while you're waiting, and have something to eat and drink. There is a canteen handy to the queue of cars and trucks. Americans will call it a *hot dog stand*. When you are not reading this book you will notice that the docking arrangements here are peculiar and ingenious — and they have to be. The Bay of Fundy has the highest tides in the world. So it takes some manoeuvring to get a semi-trailer rig onto the ferry. If you're lucky, you'll find yourself on the newer of the ferries, the *Grand Manan V*, which will remind you of a cruise ship. It is quite beautiful — and you can stand on the upper deck and take in the sunshine (if there is sunshine) and the breeze (there is almost always a breeze, sometimes a wind), and look for whales. Many people see whales. I myself never see whales, but I take the word of others that they exist. I have seen pictures. The waters around Grand Manan are a favourite feeding ground for whales.

But you're here to go bicycling, aren't you, and you may think that, because the island is comparatively small, you are going to *bicycle the island*, and thereby possess it. That you are going to ride all the roads on the island, and consequently you will know the place. Forget it. Life is more complicated than that; knowledge is more complicated than that; bicycling is more complicated than that.

In fact, you may be a touch unsettled (I was) to find that an island's isolation takes you into yourself, and there's no escaping that fact — or yourself. The experience can be good or bad, but is almost sure to be unsettling.

Of course, there are literary examples. As the beautiful little ship docks at North Head I am thinking of Alice Munro's story about Grand Manan, "Dulse." It appeared first in *The New Yorker*, and later in Alice Munro's collection of stories entitled *The Moons of Jupiter*. It is set in one of the bed and breakfasts hereabouts.

Alice Munro's central character is a woman named Lydia, an editor, who has come to the island (unnamed, but it is clear enough that it is Grand Manan) to escape the tribulations of the mainland (as you might have), which in her case means failed love. She has come to find out about herself, and she discovers a bit more than she bargained for.

At the bed and breakfast she finds herself talking to some visiting workmen. They are from the mainland, here to install telephone lines. The gentle young one offers her sex (she turns it down), and his boss offers her something different: a toughness and indifference she has never been able to acquire. A third man is also an employee of the tough fellow, but he asks nothing of Lydia and instead gives her something: he gives her dulse.

Dulse is dried seaweed. It is said to be bitter but good for you. It is produced in Grand Manan in what seems like great quantities. In Alice Munro's story, Lydia remarks that she was getting to like it and is told, "You must have made a hit." That dulse (bitter and good for you) is pretty symbolic in the story. Outside of fiction, dulse seems to be a local taste. One visitor, who *liked* Grand Manan, compared it to eating a plastic garbage bag. The fourth figure in Alice Munro's story is a minor but important character — an old American gentleman who has come to Grand Manan because of his admiration for the works of Willa Cather. Willa Cather was an American writer who came to Grand Manan every summer from 1922 through 1942 to rest and write. She is known, however, chiefly as a writer about the American West of the nineteenth century. Perhaps her best-known work (now) is the novel *Death Comes to the Archbishop*, which is set in New Mexico — and written, almost certainly, almost entirely on Grand Manan. But Willa Cather wrote virtually nothing about Grand Manan. It is as if she wanted to keep it a secret. You may soon understand why.

Alice Munro's character, Lydia, is hard on Willa Cather. Lydia is fond of the old gentleman, but he is (significantly) almost blind, and so far as Lydia is concerned, Willa Cather was no apt guide for life. When the old gentleman tells Lydia that he has encountered a local woman who once sought Willa Cather's advice on marriage, Lydia is more irritable than we might expect.

"What would she know about it, anyway?" Lydia said.

Mr. Stanley lifted his eyes from his plate and looked at her in grieved amazement.

"Willa Cather lived with a woman," Lydia said.

When Mr. Stanley answered he sounded flustered, and mildy upbraiding.

"They were devoted," he said.

"She never lived with a man."

"She knew things as an artist knows them. Not necessarily by experience."

"But what if they don't know them?" Lydia persisted.

"What if they don't?"

Alice Munro's Lydia has little patience with the romantic myths of literature, even if they are held by kindly old fellows with good intentions and good manners.

Nonetheless, you might want to think some about Willa Cather. The place where she spent her summers is on the Whistle Road. There is a small sign indicating Whale Cove Cottages. This is where Willa Cather lived (with Edith Lewis) every summer for most of the twenty years she visited Grand Manan. She liked the cottage she rented so much that when she decided to have her own cottage built, she had an exact replica erected some two hundred yards farther along the shore. She named it Orchardview. It's still there, and it still looks to be a good place to write and think in privacy.

Why did she come here? For a variation (I'd guess) on the same reason that you and I are here: weary of the zing, zing, zing of the twentieth century. She didn't like our century much. What she liked about the American West of her youth was not its newness and raw-ness, but the opportunity it seemed to offer to combine a new Edenic world with an old European culture. She liked the European immi-grants — who brought European art and civilization with them. But Willa Cather soon saw that this combination of civilization and na-ture was to be defeated everywhere in the name of Progress by the attitudes of Babbitt and the industrial mechanization of Bessemer. The century became devoted to tending its machines and making money, and its art became advertising.

A fellow can get pretty self-righteous in condemnation. I can, any-way. Then I remember that I'm riding a bicycle — the glory of the Industrial Revolution — and enjoying it very much. No Bessemer, no Bicycle.

Later, you'll probably ride to the Southwest Light and find a differ-ent kind of story. It's a lovely ride through a fishing village full of brown fish-drying sheds and out to an eighty-metre cliff hanging out over the Bay of Fundy. You'll probably want to peek over. I did. The cliffs here are towering vertical columns of basalt. They look like ruins — and are — of another time, of long ago, of an era primeval. The sea rises and slaps at the rocks and explodes in froth forever. This is what is meant by the aesthetic term *sublime*. Frightening. Why? Because the cliffs seem to require human sacrifice. They seemed to require me. I slunk away just in time.

If you want to lessen the terror, however, you might consider this story. On February 26, 1963, two brothers, Billy and Floyd Jones, set out from Maine to gather periwinkles. The engine of their motorboat failed and they drifted for twelve hours before they were driven against these cliffs by high winds. Somehow they managed to reach a kind of safety from the surf on the rocks at the base of the cliff. Billy Jones then *scaled the cliff* (you are going to find that difficult to be-lieve, but it's true) and alerted the lighthouse keeper, who called for help from Seal Cove. Among the group who arrived was the local game warden, Vernon Bagley. He volunteered to be lowered on a rope to where Floyd Jones lay unconscious on the rocks below, and on the second attempt reached him. With some difficulty the two men were dragged back up the cliffs. A year later, in the Grand Manan High School gym (it's in Grand Harbour, across from the museum where I got this story), Vernon Bagley was awarded the Carnegie Medal for Heroism.

If you're fit and interested, you might want to take a ride down to Dark Harbour. This isn't for everyone. It is a hard ride down on a gravel road and a harder ride back up it. At the bottom you'll find the basin of Dark Harbour — probably so named because the wooded hills which encircle the harbour seem to keep it always in dark shadow, and cool. You'll see a large pond at the bottom formed by the (man-made) seawall across the harbour mouth. There are fish-farming projects there now. You might see some dulse being dried on the shore. Mostly you notice the litter, the detritus of history: old planks from old ships or one old project or another, and bits of rope — bits of rope everywhere, old rope, failed rope, rope torn off and rope rotted away. Men have tried to make a hard living out of the sea here for years. If you are in Dark Harbour when the tide is going out, be prepared for another surprise on this island. Who would have thought that flat water could boil out with such violence? As if the island was suddenly tipped up, and the harbour emptied out. If the moon can drive the water this wild, what must it do to people's minds?

There's a rough life down here: a rough amphitheatre created out of what seems to be an old gravel pit, with a rough stage for concerts for anyone who wants to come. There is in fact a local festival called Dark Harbour Days, which is mostly for locals and those in the know. Not the thing for a bus tour. You'd think twice, I'd think, about bringing a bus down here full of tourists. A couple of twelve-year-old kids are taking turns driving an old car screaming along the shore to stop and spin. "Mounties don't usually come down here," they explain.

On the way back up and out along the rocky road I examine the graffiti on the rock-face. "Crystal is a Pig Fuck." Not much subtle in this ancient place. Life gets brutish in the shadows.

Finally, if you haven't found out enough about yourself from this island, you can take the free ferry from Ingalls Head (handy to the Anchorage Provincial Campground) to White Head Island. This is a short ride. *Don't put your bike in the bow of the ferry*. It will get splashed with sea water. *You've been warned!* You will be on White Head Island in about 25 minutes, and you can cycle it in another half an hour. I didn't bother to measure it. But now you'll find yourself on an island off another island, and you will discover that you are twice-removed from what you call your own time and place — an experience which you may find doubly unsettling, lonely, and a bit frightening. If you are by nature a mainlander, you'll wonder if you'll ever get back, and you may realize that of course an island is a refuge from the rest of the world, but it is also an exile and a prison. Perhaps worst of all (Napoleon would have known this on St. Helena, wouldn't he?), you are condemned to study yourself. We call this punishment.

Where to Stay

The Anchorage Provincial Campground on Route 776, which is the chief road on the island, is spacious and informal. There are 50 un-numbered sites, and you'll be told, upon checking in, to scout around and find a vacant site and park yourself. All of the sites are unserviced, but there are flush toilets and hot showers, kitchen shelters and a beach. Some of the sites (we found one) are beautifully sheltered and private. *Anchorage Provincial Campground, Seal Cove, Grand Manan, New Brunswick E0G 3B0; (506) 662-3215.*

The New Brunswick Travel Guide lists 18 bed and breakfasts on the island, as well as one motel and 11 groups of cottages. You might want to consider one of the best-known establishments, the Compass Rose, in North Head near the ferry terminal, which is especially regarded for its dining room. We had an excellent meal at the Compass Rose. *Compass Rose, North Head, Grand Manan, New Brunswick E0G 2M0; (506) 662-8570.*

The Rides

There is one major road on the island, Route 776, and it is paved — except at the very southern tip near Southwest Light. Another road is called the Back Road, and it, too, is paved. You can use a ten-speed road bike on these roads — except for the last 3 km (2 mi) or so to Southwest Light. But if you want to ride to Dark Harbour you will need a mountain bike.

I was playing Joe Spartan on this trip, but I was accompanied by Ms. Luxe, who can take to camping quite well if provided with a broad-brimmed hat, which is quite attractive, and Bill Gould and his wife Gail. We stayed at one of the most elegant of the sites in Anchorage Provincial Park. All rides are described and measured from Anchorage Provincial Park.

Ride One

Ride from the campground to the main road, Route 776, and turn left (southwest) through the fishing village of Seal Cove to the cliffs near the Southwest Light and back. There is no loop possible. You will probably want to stop coming or going to amble about among the fish-drying sheds of Seal Cove, and there is a good little restaurant, Waters Edge, which offers excellent fare at a reasonable price, accompanied (if you meet the proprietor) by superior banter.

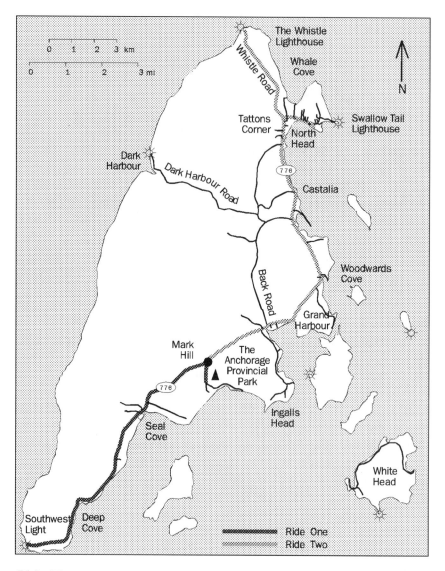

Ride Two

Leave the campground and turn right (northeast) on Route 776 and ride through Grand Harbour, Castalia and North Head to the Swallow Tail Lighthouse. You cannot cycle right to it. You will have to park your bike, descend some steps, cross a footbridge, and walk the path to the lighthouse — which looks just the way a lighthouse is supposed to look. You can walk beyond the lighthouse, if you wish, up the hill and crag where, ascending, you lose perspective and the sea and sky seem to tumble over one another. This scenic viewing is heady business. But once there, if the day is clear and the time is right, you might see the lovely ship which brought you to Grand Manan, the *Grand Manan V*, approaching the island across the calm sea. What with the tumbling sea and sky you might be reminded (well, *I* was) of W.H. Auden's poem about the people who saw "Something amazing, a boy falling out of the sky," and the ship which "Had somewhere to get to and sailed calmly on." The poem is "Musée des Beaux Arts" and the boy is Icarus.

Return to your bicycle and pedal back down Route 776 (southwest) through North Head. Two km (1.25 mi) past North Head, you will see the Whistle Road to your right (leading northwest) just opposite a drugstore. You can take a 9 km (5.5 mi) diversion up the Whistle Road past the cottages where Willa Cather lived (they are off the road at Whale Cove Cottages) to another lighthouse, where once there was a whistle to warn ships in the fog. Shipwrecks are not uncommon on Grand Manan.

Riding back down the Whistle Road to Route 776 and southerly toward the Anchorage Provincial Park, you might want to stop at the museum (full of shipwreck information and nature lore) which is across from the school on Route 776 in Grand Harbour, before returning to your campsite. Good ice cream is available at the convenience store near the school.

Ride Three

The ride to Dark Harbour requires a mountain bike and is not recommended for the novice. You want to be fit for this one.

Leave the campground and turn right (northerly) on Route 776. As you are entering Grand Harbour, look for the sign which indicates Back Road (yep, that's what it is called) and/or the airport — which, inexplicably, is not on any of the maps. But it's there; I saw it. Do we have a mystery here? Are we tracking UFOs? Is isolation getting to you, me, us?

Turn left on the Back Road. Pass by the dump. Ignore any other possible turnings, unless you want to visit the unmarked airport. Stay on the Back Road until you come to the sign indicating Dark Harbour Road leading off to your left (west). This is the only road to the west coast of the island. For a certain distance it is paved, and then it is not. You will have about 8 km (5 mi) of steep gravel road — remember to hang onto your brakes all the way down — to Dark Harbour. Then you'll have to come back up.

Return on the Dark Harbour Road to the Back Road, where (if you choose) you can cross it and continue straight on (easterly) to Casta-

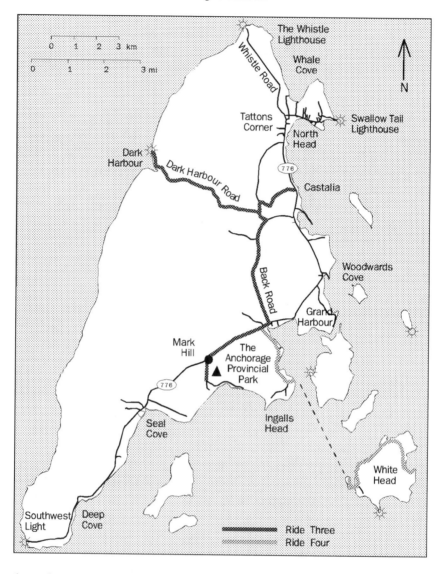

lia. Then turn right (southerly) on route 776 and return to the Anchorage Provincial Campground.

Ride Four: White Head Island

Leave the campground and turn right (northerly) on Route 776. The first right turning, in Ingalls Head, will take you to the ferry. There is a ferry sign directing you. The free ferry ride to White Head Island is 25 minutes. *Don't put your bike in the bow.* On the island you can ride from one end of the road to the other and back again for perhaps 5 km (3 mi).

ST. ANDREWS

DISTANCE: 20 km (12 mi)	**DIFFICULTY:** Easy
TIME: 1 hr	

Scandalous Behaviour

St. Andrews is a theatrical little town which could easily be the set for a Disney film about family values and good kids and happy dogs (all of which might exist there, of course), but that is only a first impression. In fact, there are at least two other towns in the same space, and even a third. One is the old Loyalist settlement, full of colonial architecture (the courthouse is a grand example), and small houses of balance and symmetry, perfectly proportional to the trees and churches. Great sense of proportion in the eighteenth century. We seem to have lost it entirely.

But on top of that Loyalist town is the town of the Wealthy. The Algonquin Hotel is its cathedral, and Ministers Island is its secular domain. Ministers Island was owned by Sir William Van Horne, who built the Canadian Pacific Railway. He was a big man and he built big: outsize barn, outsize house. The hotel and the railway together brought in the Wealthy for the summer. You can read about them in a book full of curiosities and memories by Willa Walker: *No Hay Fever and a Railway*. The Wealthy brought their families here for summering and meeting one another with the usual intention that they would marry one another, which they quite frequently did. No wonder that St. Andrews-By-the-Sea (the name on the railway advertising poster) is like no place else in New Brunswick. Willa Walker remembers that everyone in town went swimming at Katy's Cove, but that the Wealthy swam in the morning, and the Others (who frequently worked in the hotel) swam in the afternoon. It was understood that they did not immerse in common water. She points out that the practice seems silly now, but it was natural enough then.

It is Willa Walker who points toward the literary side of St. Andrews. She and her husband moved here (where she had summered) in 1948. In Ottawa before the Second World War, David Walker had been ADC to Governor-General Lord Tweedsmuir (John Buchan), author of *The Thirty-nine Steps*. Captured by the Germans, Walker was part of the daring escape from Warburg prison, but, captured again, he spent a good part of the war as a POW at the infamous Colditz prison camp. In St. Andrews, he wrote the best-seller *Geordie*, which became an equally popular film, and several other books, culminating in his memoir, *Lean Wind, Lean.*

However, the major reason I'm here is that the great Belgian/French author, Georges Simenon, lived here for about six months in 1946. Not long, you say? No, except that for Simenon six months was time enough to knock off four novels, if he wished. What's more, they would be *good* novels — about the anguish of the human heart, usually, and the results of terrible passions — often set in seaside towns. He liked seaside towns, seaside villages. That is the third St. Andrews, and the one to which he was likely attracted. There is a small fishing fleet, still, which brings lobster to the town wharf.

But it is the passion which interests me. Simenon was living *ménage à trois* at 126 Reed Avenue. A surprising house: doesn't look grand enough for his talent or passions or subsequent international fame and critical acclaim. He was even then a very successful writer (the creator of Inspector Maigret) and became one of the wealthiest writers in the world. Deserved every penny, too. I recommend *La chambre bleue (The Blue Room)* and *L'Ours en peluche (Teddy Bear).*

Simenon recalls in one of his memoirs how he flew out of Saint John, New Brunswick, on the day of the nuclear test on Bikini Atoll in the Pacific. Everyone was afraid to fly that day but he wasn't, much. Nothing happened. The plane went where it was supposed to go. He went to Montreal and bought a used car and returned to Saint Andrews and later left for the States with wife and secretary and son. Still later he married the secretary (who was from Ottawa), who gave him great delight and even greater grief.

The house seems to have two front doors. It may have been that which appealed to him. It fit his family situation at the time. Now the home and office of a veterinarian, it is just across from the entrance to the golf links of the Algonquin Hotel. Simenon recalls taking his son to the Huntsman Marine Laboratory and Aquarium to see the seals. You can go there, too.

You will certainly want to ride the streets of the town. They are lovely: leafy and shaded and quiet. The Loyalist houses sit harmoniously in a world which is just the right size. The mansions are interesting, too, and quite often imposing: gate posts are frequent; there are sometimes wrought-iron gates. There might be a sign: NO

TRESPASSING. Stop here to worship the example of Private Property. Have your photograph taken in front of the gates; make sure the sign is evident.

Where to Stay

The Passamaquoddy Park Campground is operated by the Kiwanis Club of St. Andrews, and is located in the town on Indian Point Road, which is Route 127, right across from Passamaquoddy Bay. It has hot showers and flush toilets and is of course handy to everything in town. *Passamaquoddy Park Campground, Box 116, St. Andrews, New Brunswick E0G 2X0; (506) 529-3439.*

There are many motels and bed and breakfast establishments in the St. Andrews area, some with most excellent reputations, but if you are considering an alternative to camping, you might want to go to the other extreme and hang about with Willa Walker's summer people (practise your golf swing from time to time and look into the distance; mention a fondness for obscure single-malt scotches) at the Algonquin Hotel. Take tea on the long verandah. Its simple address speaks volumes. *Algonquin Hotel, St. Andrews, New Brunswick E0G 2X0; (506) 529-8823; fax (506) 529-4194; (800)-268-9411 (Canada); (800)-828-7447 (U.S.)*

The Ride

This is not a long ride, and most any bicycle will do, but a mountain bike is recommended. It starts at the Blockhouse parking lot, which is on Brandy Cove Road, which is an extension northwesterly of Water Street, which is the main street of St. Andrews. The Block-house was built to repel Americans, but this did not turn out to be necessary.

Leave the parking lot of the Blockhouse, turn left on Brandy Cove Road and ride in a northwesterly direction up a little hill toward the golf course. The first side road on your left says Dead End, and is. Pass by it. You have turned onto Cedar Lane because you cannot do anything else. Take the next side road left, northwesterly, toward the Huntsman Marine Laboratory, museum and Aquarium. You will be cycling *through* the golf course (aren't you glad you're wearing a helmet?), down the hill, around a bend, and there you are: the Huntsman Marine Laboratory, Museum and Aquarium. You can pay a fee and look at the marine life. Return up the steep little granny-gear hill you recently descended, and at the top of the hill, just before the golf course from this direction, turn left, northeasterly, into the residence

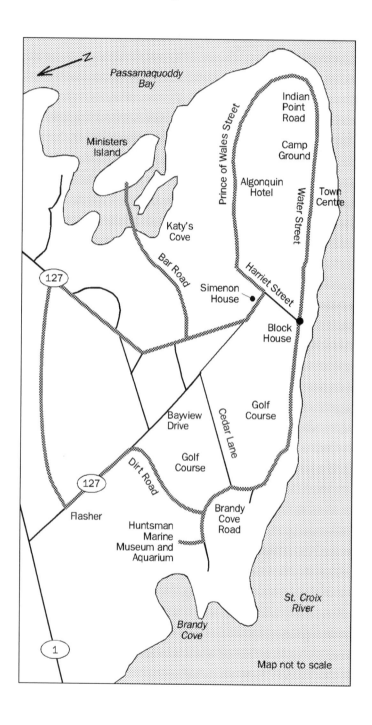

complex of the Huntsman Marine Laboratory. You turn just in front of a lovely elegant old eighteenth century sort of building which should house Jane Austen, but in fact it is called the Anderson Residence for students, and the name over the door is LinksCrest. This figures: St. Andrews, golf. . . .

Cycle through the compound and take the dirt road you will see leading away from it on the other side. Watch out for low tree branches! (Aren't you glad you're wearing a helmet?) The T will be the junction with paved Route 127. Turn left on the paved Route 127 and ride northwesterly and turn right at the flasher. You will ride cross-country and meet Route 127 again. (Route 127 makes a V in St. Andrews; you have just crossed the gap of the V.) Turn right, south-westerly, on Route 127 and ride to the Bar Road. Turn left, easterly, on the Bar Road. The is a *bar* as in "Crossing the Bar." Alfred, Lord Tennyson. Remember? The bar is the causeway to Ministers Island. You can cross only at low tide. The St. Andrews Chamber of Commerce has very kindly and very wisely posted the tide times so there will be no excuse whatever if you are caught over there. Getting there — across the bar — is hard work: the bar is loose, deep, shifting gravel which will throw you off your bike in a moment. You would be wise to dismount and push. I did.

On the other side of the bar you will see NO TRESPASSING signs, which means that some people will hide their bikes and go up the road anyway to see the deer. Remember how the seventeenth century French aristocrats always wanted deer in their parks? Deer somehow went with pastoral delights and dressing up to play in haystacks.

You can pay for a proper tour of Ministers Island. Enquire at the tourist information kiosk at the wharf in St. Andrews. Another tourist information kiosk is located at the junction of Route 1 and Route 127.

Ride back on the Bar Road to Route 127 and turn left, southwesterly; Route 127 joins Reed Avenue. Turn left on Reed Avenue, past the one-time residence of Georges Simenon and the Algonquin Golf Course, and turn left onto Harriet Street and ride up and turn right past the stately Algonquin Hotel. You are on Prince of Wales Street. Ride this street downhill, and around the curve you will find yourself back on Indian Point Road, riding northwesterly toward the Passamaquoddy Park Campground. If you continue past the campground on Water Street and go straight (careful of the intersection at Harriet Street), you will find yourself at the Blockhouse again.

Dogs and Other Adversaries

Cyclists as a species have few natural enemies. Well, *yahoos* of course. You see them on the roads grunting and farting their mufflers and waving middle fingers as expressively as they can and yowling their minds' dearest wonders, but aside from them, there are only three complicating factors in a cyclist's life.

1. Headwinds. There is nothing to be done about headwinds except boast about them. "Boy, that was some stiff wind off the water, eh? Had to gear down and *pedal* downhill." Listeners will nod; listening cyclists will understand. Cycling encourages the basic virtues of plugging along, hanging in, enduring — and triumphing at last over adverse conditions. We are Horatio Algers and Nancy Drews on wheels.

2. Dump Trucks. Or Logging Trucks. One's as bad as the other. Big bad uncaring nasty creatures who look upon cyclists as annoying bugs. Worse, these beasts are encountered usually on country roads where all travellers are bouncing along together over the ruts. The working beast, moreover, resents the blithe spirit of the cycling creature, and not infrequently seeks ways of demonstrating that moral disapproval from on high. If we meet in the old folks home, I shall personally kill some of these guys. I think I'll use poison.

3. Dogs. O yes. Dogs. It ought be said immediately that I am as a rule fond of dogs. I have known many dogs. I have lived with dogs, and dogs have lived with me, in long and amicable relationships. Among dogs I am known as an uncommon good hand with ears. Dogs have been known to drop their drooling heads in my lap unbidden and content. Dogs and I look soulfully at one another in understanding.

And, cycling, I have come to know more about dogs than previously. I have developed an eye for breeds and ancestry, as you may have. Retriever dogs, for instance, do not usually have any interest whatsoever in cyclists. A retriever's job is to go fetch recently deceased birds from the water, and retrievers are very good at that and understandably proud of their abilities. They commonly have soft mouths and look upon biting with distaste.

Then there are short yappy dogs who must make up for their lack of size in bark and repetitition of bark. These dogs can go into frenzies of seemingly sincere hatred in which mouth and tail (not infrequently docked) thrash in unison. These are perhaps the only dogs capable of barking and leaping straight up in the air at the same moment. I look upon them without serious annoyance — because I know full well that even if they are loose, they are too damned short to reach up and bite me. Safe from their impotent fury, I can be quite benign about these dogs.

But there are also dogs whose ancestry tells a different story, a story which says they ought to leap upon deer and drag them down and eat them, and these dogs — distinguished by the long narrow muzzle for getting into the abdominal cavity and savaging the guts — are to be considered with some circumspection. You on your bicycle are surprisingly like a deer. These dogs are bad enough one at a time, but a pair can be thoroughly disconcerting, and more than a pair I do not wish to consider.

In point of fact, however, most dogs do not want to eat you. Quite frequently, the dog you encounter merely wants to warn you off its territory. Such a dog might well sprint alongside the road barking like hell until it reaches the boundaries of its property line (the dog knows exactly where it is), whereupon it will return to home base swaggering its butt in satisfaction. You've been warned off; a good job has been done.

So in fact the cyclist soon learns to know the dog's intention at a glance. The cyclist learns to read the dog's gesture, just as we learn to read human gestures — and the dog learns that the cyclist's peculiar rolling movement is nothing except kind of odd. You can tell pretty quickly when a dog has meanness on his mind.

As you can learn very quickly how to distinguish the bark of a dog who is tied up from one who is loose. Of course, the adrenaline still shoots through your frame at the first fierce bark (the adrenaline can get you extra speed and quite remarkable extra distance from your legs), but you soon realize that the loudest bark is probably from the chained dog, who is frightened because he or she is chained, and therefore vulnerable. You learn very quickly to look for chains where you see a doghouse — and for bicycles in the yard. If there are bicycles it is likely that the family dog doesn't give a damn about you using his road.

But be wary of rural poverty. In my experience, more than three wrecked cars around a trailer signifies two mean dogs. Their meanness demonstrates the ancient rule: those who have nothing worth stealing are sure that everybody wants to steal what little they have. This applies to both dogs and humans.

But how do you deal with a dog that comes after you?

I once carried a short club — but one day when I was escaping from a property-line dog the club fell from my bike, and when I looked back I saw the dog nosing it and realized he was going to take it home to play with, and I never carried a club after that.

A good method might be that suggested to me by a touring cyclist I met in Nova Scotia, who sprayed the attacking dog between the eyes with water from her water bottle. She said he was so surprised he stopped dead in his tracks and walked away. Hurt dignity, probably. Never underestimate your power to wound dignity. (Applies to humans as well as dogs.)

I myself carry a product endorsed by the U.S. Postal Service for dealing with bad dogs. You cannot legally bring this product across the border into Canada and I have no idea how I acquired it. But I have never used it.

But, as I discovered riding from Pugwash to Wallace, I mostly rely on my voice — and my ancestry, which is, not to put too fine a point on it, in good part hillbilly. I say "Git, git, *git!*" and I mean it. The vowel speaks experience, practice. I come from generations of men who take no guff from dogs, and much as we like dogs, never consider them substitute humans (damned insulting to the dog, if you ask me) and, moreover, are quite willing to grab the said beast by the ears to come to a symbiotic understanding. Not that it is necessary, you understand. The dog knows the word *"Git!"* It's in the blood-memory of the species, probably from the day dogs and humans began to share caves and supper.

But in fact the usual advice when you are faced with an attacking dog — it's good advice — is to get off your bike and keep the bike between you and him until somebody comes to call him off or he gets bored and goes home. Let him try to devour your chainwheel. That'll teach him.

It is likely, however, that you will not encounter a single mean dog on the rides listed in this book. I met only one, and he's dead and gone. Many of the rides are through dairy country — and dairycountry is especially good for cyclists, because in dairy country dogs are kept tied or occupied with cows. Association with cows somehow invokes a kind of laid-back life. There are, in fact, dogs you will meet while cycling who are quite endearing. Not that you exactly meet them. You catch sight of them sleeping in the sun, lazing about the house, sprawled on the front steps. These are retired dogs. They do not want to make the effort of dealing with you.

You can see the retired dog and the retired dog can see you, but the two sightings of one another must be at different moments. Should you lock eyes, the dog will have to bark. If he has to bark, he will have to use energy. A good bark requires the use of the entire body; the whole body shakes; it can wear a fellow out for days and days and days.

So the retired dog soon learns not to make eye contact. Oh, he knows you are on the road. He's not blind, not deaf yet, and has some powers of nose remaining. But he is careful not to look you in the eye. No, he will gaze out over the field away from the road to see what dangers might be lurking there, and consider the height of the hills beyond, or he will examine the leaf between his feet for new and surprising properties until you are far down the road, and he will sigh deeply.

You might safely look back then, and see his eyes on you, thinking long thoughts of the wonders of the world: cyclists! Whatever next? Then he goes back to sleep.

BLISSVILLE

DISTANCE: 50 km (31 mi)	**DIFFICULTY:** Moderate
TIME: 2 hr 30 min	**OTHER FACTORS:** Rough roads

Biking Through Blissville

In fact, this is a trip through Blissville to Elsewhere. It is not your usual ride. This ride begins with poetry.

More beautiful and soft than any moth
With burring furred antennae feeling its huge path
Through dusk, the air-liner with shut-off engines
Glides over suburbs and the sleeves set trailing tall
To point the wind. Gently, broadly, she falls,
Scarcely disturbing charted currents of air.

Those are the opening lines of Stephen Spender's poem, "The Landscape Near An Aerodrome." British, you will notice, but appropriate for this ride to Elsewhere.

Elsewhere, because I intended to start this ride at the old terminal building of the Blissville Air Field, but the terminal isn't there anymore. Nothing's there anymore but a deteriorating landing strip which belongs to CFB Gagetown, fenced and forbidden, noted *DÉFENSE DE PASSER* (more threatening, somehow, in French), and ghosts — of planes past and passengers. It turns out that Blissville was not primarily a Second World War military training field, nor a spray-plane field, although it has served for both, but was instead the major airfield for airline service in and out of central New Brunswick prior to 1950. Trans-Canada Airlines (TCA) flew in and out of here with twin-engined Lockheed 10s and 12s and the famous DC-3s. ("More beautiful and soft than any moth/ With burring furred antennae feeling its huge path . . . ") You took the train north from Saint John or south from Fredericton to nearby Fredericton Junction. Then you were borne away by those great moths elsewhere. Now there is nothing here but Elsewhere.

Elsewhere is sometimes Memory. I'm a sucker for old airfields (you may have noticed), and I remember the beauty of a DC-3 coming in to set down gently on the runway, hanging lightly in the air.

Sometimes Elsewhere is Beauty. This is a beautiful ride, especially in autumn, and I am riding this route in autumn, and recommend it especially for autumn. New Brunswick Tourism will tell you with very little prompting that, for the last couple of weeks in September and the first couple of weeks in October, New Brunswick is the most stunningly beautiful place in the world. All those trees, you see. All those trees changing into gold and red. And in autumn, of course, the air is cool and the bugs have gone. A perfect time to ride through the woodlands and along rivers and past lakes.

Elsewhere, however, is not always Edenic. On this ride also I met the Fascist Beast. But you can't be intimidated, can you? Courage, like Freedom — as Charlie Brown remarks — must be asserted every day. Nowhere in the world (not even Elsewhere) is without threat or evil. The Fascist Beast was a very beautiful Doberman. Never mind. By the time you ride this route he may have died, possibly of natural causes.

[Stop Press. The Dog is Dead. Not of natural causes.]

So you are cycling through Blissville — which, you may notice, is in one sense little more than a name of a railway crossing, some few houses, a church — on your way to Elsewhere, which you find frequently on your bicycle, singing along. Elsewhere is sometimes the unvoiced laughter of joy. You feel it in your legs, in the wind in your face. Elsewhere is the breeze sighing in the trees, the scent of crisp leaf in autumn, the wild colours, the centrifugal force which holds you firm as you bend into a curve. Elsewhere is cheerful exhaustion. Elsewhere is poetry; Elsewhere is the river, serene as a Modigliani sleeping nude. Elsewhere is Art. Elsewhere is where you go on your bicycle in circles.

And no, dammit, I will not be embarrassed by poetry in a cycling guide. You coming with me, or not?

Where to Stay

There are no handy accommodations to this loop. I drove to it from Fredericton (about 35 km [21 mi]).

The Sunbury-Oromocto Provincial Park campground (with the necessary amenities) is 13 km (8 mi) north of the suggested cycling loop, and if you ride from here you will add 26 km (16 mi) of annoying traffic to the loop. The Park is on the Waterville Road and you can reach it via Routes 660 and 7 if you are just arriving in the area. There are several signs directing you from both roads, but getting there requires some twisting and turning; pay attention. *Sunbury-Oromocto Provincial Park, R.R. #3, Oromocto, New Brunswick E2V 2G3; (506) 357-3708.*

The Ride

You will want a mountain bike for this ride — although a hybrid might do.

I began from the parking lot of the Blissville United Baptist Church (established 1833) on Route 101. I rode north from Blissville on Route 101 to the junction of Routes 101 and 660, and stayed on 101 (left, westerly) to Fredericton Junction — a distance of some 8 km (5 mi) from the church parking lot. I turned right (north) on the Wilsey Road (which is marked with a street sign) at the Irving station. The Wilsey Road inexplicably becomes the Post Road just outside Fredericton Junction and turns to dirt. The dirt Post Road is full of potholes, but you will dance nimbly among them.

Turn right (northeasterly) on the DeWitt Road. You have to watch for this because, from this direction, there is no sign. It is the first major turning to your right, however, with any kind of sign at all on this road. To feel sure, ride through the junction, stop, and turn around: you'll see the sign which says DeWitt Road. Take it the only direction you can (easterly) and ride on the dirt for about 2.5 km (1.5 mi) to a little rise which meets a paved surface, which is the unidentified Sunpoke Road. Turn right, easterly, and get up speed going downhill in case the damned Fascist Beast (*since deceased!*) is loose, and zip down over the tracks to a tidy little building with mailboxes where you can stop and contemplate life and eat the muffins you have brought with you. I did. This is Rusagonis Station. Once you could catch a train from here to Fredericton. Now you can't. This is called progress. Follow the road (you have no choice) southerly. It almost immediately turns to dirt and you want to bear left (easterly) through the marshland around the foot of Sunpoke Lake. Past the marshland you'll find yourself cycling northward alongside the serene Oromocto River. The road makes a right turn across a bridge, and now you are in a neat little community called French Lake. The cemetery on your right is the Wood Cemetery. Take the left fork and climb the short hill, and turn right at the church. You are now riding easterly on the French Lake Road, which has a chipseal surface, and, ignoring New Road to your left, continue to the junction with Route 660. Turn right (southerly) on Route 660 and, with Base Gagetown — one of the largest military training bases in the world — to your left, ride 15 km (9 mi) until you come to the junction of 660 and 101. You have been here before. Continue south on 101 until you come to the parking lot of Blissville United Baptist Church.

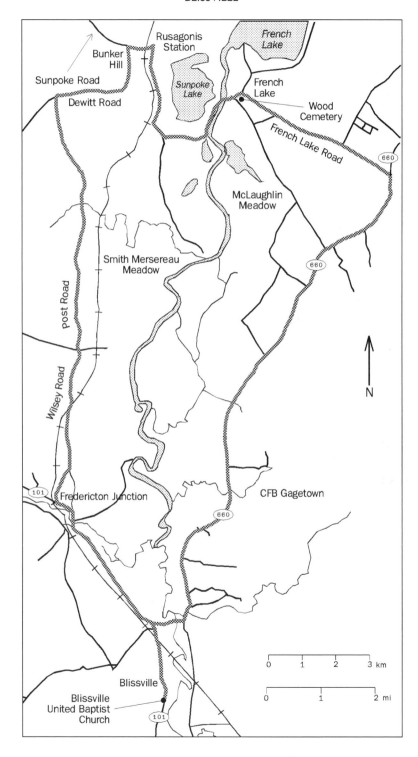

Bunker Hill

Rusagonis Station

French Lake

Sunpoke Road

Sunpoke Lake

French Lake

Dewitt Road

Wood Cemetery

French Lake Road

660

McLaughlin Meadow

660

Smith Mersereau Meadow

Post Road

Wilsey Road

N

101

Fredericton Junction

CFB Gagetown

660

0   1   2   3 km

0   1   2 mi

Blissville

Blissville United Baptist Church

101

HARVEY LAKE

DISTANCE: 54 km (34 mi)	**OTHER FACTORS:** Low gear
TIME: 3 hrs	hills; steep downhill into
DIFFICULTY: Moderate to Difficult	Harvey Station.

Heartless Young Men

I am prejudiced of course, but to my mind, the single triumph of the Industrial Revolution was the bicycle. It was and is perhaps the perfect machine: it can convey more weight at a higher speed with less energy than any other gadget ever created, and it is powered solely by human verve. Wonderful. Amazing. Think about it. Humans are wickedly clever creatures, no?

Yes. And the invention of the bicycle meant that poor folks, working folks, folks who could not afford a horse (the upkeep is tremendous; ask anyone who owns one) had cheap transportation available to them, and they took advantage of it. Off they cycled across the hills and through the valleys of the turn of the century (we are riding here through the turn of the century) to the next village, the next town, the opposite gender. The bicycle played a role in courting.

The results were not always salutary. For example, here's a story with a nasty little twist at the end. Don't blame the bicycle: I have no idea if the participants in this story had bicycles or not. Did Adam? Did Eve? Humans are such wicked creatures; young men are fickle.

You'll find the story in the cemetery of the Lake George United Church. You will have to take a sprout off your loop to discover it. The story is on the gravestone of young Roxie Hoyt, who died on 22 September 1916, at the age of 18. She died of despair and unhappiness and left this world with vengeance in her heart. You can read about it:

> *IN THIS COLD GRAVE*
> *I LIE. I WAS TOO*
> *YOUNG TO DIE.*
> *YOUNG FRIENDS:*
> *I WAS NOT TO*
> *BLAME TO DES-*
> *TROY MY LIFE IT*
> *WAS HIS AIM.*

HERE IS MY
DECEIVER'S NAME

WE KNOW THAT
GOD IS JUST
AND TRUE
AND WILL GIVE
THIS BOLD WRETCH
HIS DUE

There's poetry. But you'll notice that the name she promised is absent. That's the second part of the story. According to local telling, the alleged Deceiver or his family stole Roxie's gravestone more than once and threw it into Lake George. Each time, it was retrieved and re-erected for all to see and know. Finally, the fellow came in the night with a chisel to save himself from further shame. It's a crude job, but enough. You can see his work for yourself.

Turn away from the graveyard and take in the vista of the New Brunswick countryside, the fields sloping down to the lake. It is not difficult (is it?) to imagine the fellow and Roxie walking down there into the shadows of the trees.

But, back on the road, you'll find yourself cycling through country which in the nineteenth century was alive with rural life. You will see farms which have been roughened by every winter since, and evidence of communities which are no more: nothing remains but a schoolhouse — now called a "community hall," and not much used from the look of it — and perhaps the shell of an old church, and (always) a cemetery.

There is some lowland, much like a swamp, where you might expect to see a Moose. If you do, STOP! Keep your distance. A Moose may be a comic figure in a TV cartoon or strolling across the screen in your living room, but in actual fact the Moose is a huge, dim-witted, ill-tempered beast, and *every year several people in these parts are either killed or maimed in collisions between Moose and automobile. The Moose, even if it dies, always wins!*

But likely you won't see one. Moose like to wade in swamps and you are zipping along the road through the forest primeval. Suddenly a pasture appears, and you will be surprised at how welcome you find this sign of human accomplishment.

There is even a railway line to cross (think of the nineteenth century life which the railway engendered — the farmers leaving off their butter, milk cans, crates of eggs at the station; the station is no more), and you will discover, as well, the tidy little nineteenth century industrial community of York Mills, which is not quite populous enough to warrant the term *village*. There is, however, a mill race, and — surprise! — the still-functioning enterprise of Briggs & Little Yarn and Wool. You can go into the shop, if you're there at the right time of day. You can buy wool if you knit or for friends who knit. You can inhale the warm comfort of the aroma of wool. Or you can step outside and stare down into the turbulent waters of the mill-race and think long thoughts of human frailty and trusting girls and wicked young men.

Where to Stay

It was a day trip out of Fredericton for me, but if you want to settle for a bit you have a choice of two campgrounds and one bed and breakfast, all of them on the loop.

Lake George Provincial Park is 11 km off the Trans-Canada on Route 636, north of Harvey. (A note on local terminology. This community is generally referred to locally as *Harvey*. But there is another community called Harvey down yon beyond Fundy National Park, and in fact the official name of this large village on Route 3 is *Harvey Station*.) You can reach the Lake George Provincial Park by turning off the Trans-Canada (on 635, then south on 636) or by driving north from Harvey on Route 636. There is a beach and shade, and hot showers and flush toilets. *Lake George Provincial Park, R.R. #3, Harvey Station, New Brunswick E0H 1H0; (506) 366-2933.*

Little's Lakeshore Campground is a privately operated establishment, some 5 km off Route 3 west of Harvey Station. It has shade, hot showers, flush toilets, and a beach on Harvey Lake. *Little's Lakeshore Campground, R.R. #4, Harvey Station, New Brunswick E0H 1H0; (506) 366-2822.*

The bed and breakfast is Myrna's Manor, right on Route 3, between York Mills and Harvey Station. *Myrna's Manor, R.R. #4, Harvey Station, New Brunswick E0H 1H0; (506) 366-3127.*

The Ride

A mountain bike or a hybrid would be best for this loop, but because all of it is paved, it is also suitable for a ten-speed.

You can of course begin anywhere on the loop, but I began at the Lake George Provincial Campground and rode northerly on Route 636 to the junction with 635. The gravestone diversion will take you

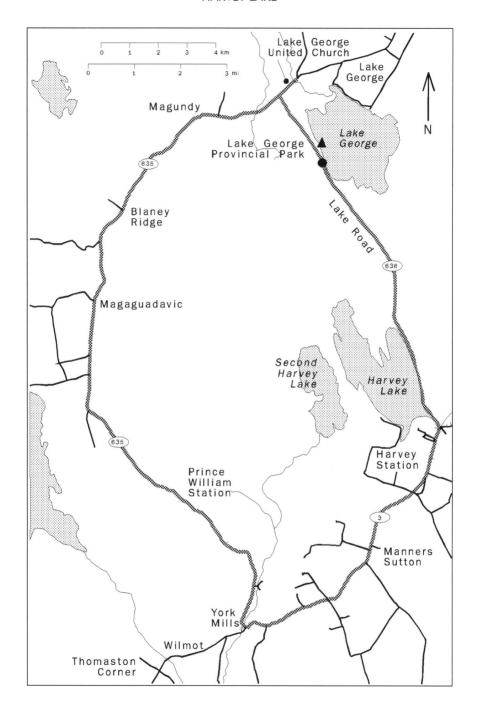

right (easterly) on Route 635 to the Lake George United Church, a distance of no more than 2 km. After contemplation of life's cruelties, you will want to return to the junction of Route 635 and 636 and take 635 westerly on a long curve of approximately 26 km (16 mi) to York Mills and Route 3. Turn left (northeasterly) on Route 3 toward Harvey Station, a distance of 11 km (7 mi). This stretch of road can be heavily travelled at certain times of the year, but the shoulder is firm and gravelled, and not bad at all for a mountain bike. Approaching Harvey Station there is a long steep downhill. *Remember to apply your brakes all the way down.* In Harvey Station you will turn left (northerly) on Route 636 to return to Lake George Provincial Park, a distance of some 13 km (8 mi).

MACTAQUAC COUNTRY and HOLLAND FALLS

DISTANCE: 37 km (23 mi) to Mactaquac Provincial Park, 47 km (30 mi) to Kingsclear Resort Hotel
TIME: 2 hrs to Mactaquac Provincial Park, 2 hrs 30 min to Kingsclear Resort Hotel
DIFFICULTY: Moderate to Difficult

OTHER FACTORS: If you ride this loop counter-clockwise (as indicated), you will escape any serious uphills. But the dirt roads are sometimes rough and challenging.

Pagan Rites

People like to worship water, don't they? At the seaside, they stand and look out to sea, admiring vastness, distance, horizon. At a dam they look at light playing through the curtain of water, flashing. They look at light in water and think (perhaps) about glass, about diamonds.

Here at Holland Falls the joys are simpler and more individual. You look up at the water spilling out from the cleft rock overhead and you must fight the desire to strip naked and step under, to cry out, sing, and sacrifice an ear of corn.

In my case, mind you, resistance was made easier by the time of year. It was autumn. The water was damned cold; there was a chill in the air — and, to be honest, I'd been humming along the roads with friend and guide (actor, lawyer, athlete) Bill Gould (he once lived hereabouts), thinking about the glories of autumn. New Brunswick is astonishingly beautiful in late September and early October. It is worth scheduling your trip here to take advantage of the beauties. Besides, most of the other visitors have returned home by autumn, and neither the roads nor the inns are crowded at the end of the season. In late September and early October you can feel wealthy (and possibly noble) just by being outdoors, surrounded by gold leaf. You might find yourself musing on the values of gold — why humanity has always valued that particular colour. Read Keats: "To Autumn."

But in high summer the attraction of a waterfall is nigh irresistible. Holland Falls is a bit off the road and not marked, so it has the added attraction of a kind of secrecy. You'll have to pay close attention to your instructions. But you can park your bike at the top of the hill and make your way down the dark path through the trees to the sound of falling water, and at the bottom you'll see evidence of the small neat fires of other worshippers — and an old millstone. The millstone may remind you that the countryside was once a place of much more commercial activity than it is now. Post a guard at the top of the path and expose yourself to a greater or lesser extent to falling water . . . or dip your hand in . . . or content yourself with removing your shoes; stick your feet in the churned water. Wiggle your toes. Water is worth the worship.

It is, isn't it? If you weren't that sort of person you wouldn't be out here spinning with the earth, would you?

Where to Stay

There are three campgrounds nearby — one provincial and two private. Each has its virtues and all are on the loop.

Mactaquac Provincial Park is on Route 105, which you will probably reach by leaving the Trans-Canada Highway and crossing the dam; follow the signs. This is a large provincial park (300 sites) with the usual hot showers and flush toilets and extensive recreational facilities as well, including a beach, a golf course and hiking trails. *Mactaquac Provincial Park, Mactaquac, New Brunswick E0H 1P0; (506) 363-3011.*

Simpler, but certainly well equipped (flush toilets, showers, grocery), is the Heritage Farm Campground, which is 10 km (6 mi) west of Mactaquac Park on Route 105. *Heritage Farm Campground, R.R. #1, Mouth of Keswick, New Brunswick E0H 1N0; (506) 363-2119.*

Everetts Campground is right on the Mactaquac headpond on Route 105. It has flush toilets and hot showers and 32 sites. *Everetts Campground, R. R. #1, Mouth of Keswick, New Brunswick E0H 1N0; (506) 363-2770.*

The Kingsclear Hotel and Resort is a recently built four-star establishment with aspirations to contemporary elegance. Right off the Trans-Canada Highway, it offers not only hotel accommodation, but cottages as well, and (in the past, anyway) a sometimes ambitious dining room. It is 5 km (3 mi) from Mactaquac Provincial Park, but it is listed under Fredericton in the New Brunswick Accommodation Guide. It is approximately 20 km (12 mi) from Fredericton. *Kingsclear Hotel & Resort, R.R. #6, Fredericton, New Brunswick E3B 4X7; (506) 363-5111; fax (506) 363-3000; (800)-561-5111.*

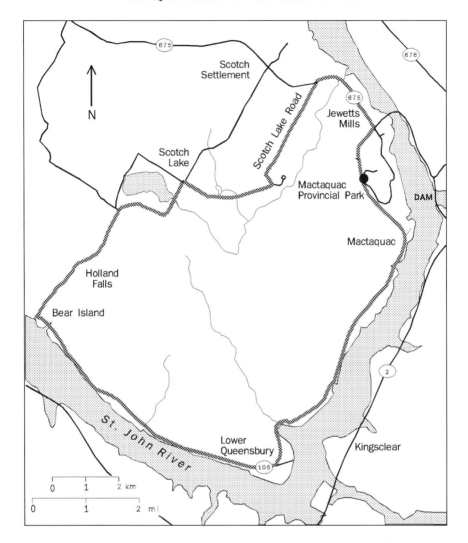

The Ride

You will need a mountain bicycle for this route.

Bill Gould and I began from the parking lot of the Mactaquac Provincial Park Golf Course. You might want to do the same.

At the exit of the park, turn right (easterly) on Route 105 in the direction of Kingsclear. After only 2 km (1 mi), at the junction with Route 615 at the place designated Jewetts Mills (there is a sign by the Shell station convenience store), turn left (northwesterly) on Route

615. Follow this paved road past the cemetery on the right and turn left (southwesterly) just past the cemetery onto the Scotch Lake Road. There is a sign: Scotch Lake Road. Here you will encounter the only serious uphill on the loop. The Scotch Lake Road makes a zig-zag into farm country. Stay with zig and zag. (If you make a mistake and zip off onto a misleading dirt road, you'll find yourself in a farm-yard and will have to return.) But if you stay with the zig left and the zag right, you will find yourself immediately on a washboard dirt sur-face. Hang on. The road surface improves but does not change its nature. You will take the first left turning after the zigzag, and it is easily missed. If you come to a sign reading Scotch Lake Cemetery, *you have gone 400 yards too far.* Return to what may look like a log-ging road going downhill into the woods. In the distance (to your right) you can see Scotch Lake. This is a fine vista before you disap-pear into a tunnel of trees on a road which, clearly enough, serves sometimes as a creek bed. Oh, the joys of hopping around on a moun-tain bike and dodging the rocks and slewing through the fine sand which someone has considerately put out in what might have other-wise been bogs and puddles. Continue this wilderness riding until you come to a Y junction. Bear left, southwest, toward the St. John River.

The road is now a better grade of dirt and mostly downhill, and you will indeed be flying down the ridge toward the St. John River when you come to a small concrete bridge. Slow down. Twenty-five yards beyond the bridge, up a rise, on your left — look for signs of cars having been parked — is the entrance to Holland Falls. Lock your bike at the top and make your way down to the falls.

Back on the road, continue to fly downhill (southwesterly) toward the St. John River to the junction with Route 105. You are at Bear Is-land. You will see the designation on a couple of buildings. Turn left (southeasterly) on Route 105 and ride back to Mactaquac Provincial Park.

A Serious Case of Mistaken Identity

Bill Gould and I were bouncing down that wonderful dirt road which doubles as a creek bed, and having just a wonderful time, when we came to the Y junction which would take us back toward the St. John River. At the Y junction is a tidy little house, and out in front, gambolling about in joyful abandon, entertaining the woman who was its possessor, was a cheerful little pony.

I thought, what a pleasant scene — a pony at play.

Then the pony spied us and said Woof! and I realized I had made a serious error in identification. Biggest damn dog I've ever seen. Came out to look us over seriously, and we were staring eyeball to eyeball with the offspring of a Doberman and a Great Dane. He in turn was staring at the hard-shelled heads of two of the biggest, most complicated insects he'd ever seen. We were quickly and deeply into a demonstration of the importance of mutual identification, and then into a matter of existential decision. He had a choice to make. Which of us was he going to eat?

Fortunately, he was defeated by the conflicting attractions inherent in the philosophical problem, and his owner said "Yo! Dog!" and we sang by in top gear. Glancing over my shoulder some distance down the road (amazing the speed you can get out of a mountain bike, sometimes), I saw that the Great Beast had returned to gambolling about in the front yard. Why, nothing but a big puppy at play, that's all, simply looking after his territorial interests. Just a cheerful adolescent, that's all.

May he maintain his equanimity forever, and bear no malice toward large hard-shelled insects on wheels to the end of his days!

THE ST. JOHN RIVER

DISTANCE: 54 km (33.5 mi)	**OTHER FACTORS:** Some right
TIME: 4 hrs	bodacious hills. Carry food and
DIFFICULTY: Difficult	water.

Cool Water

Ain't life a wonder, though?

I mean: here I am, cycling up over the hills which overlook the broad and wonderful St. John River north of Belleisle Bay — and I am riding in autumn and the air is crisp and the trees are red and gold, and the scenery is almost too beautiful to bear and I am thinking about apples — and later I find that one of the great mythologizers of the American *West* was born right near here, right near Hatfield Point, in 1908. That's a real oddity. He lived here until he was eighteen, but what he saw in his head was the vast flat West. He wrote cowboy poetry in high school, it seems. And perhaps he convinced his family that the western landscape was more important than this one (how? this is wonderful!), and his family took off for Arizona. Later the young fellow — name of Bob Nobles — went to California, where he hooked up with a singing group and a fellow from Ohio who was equally smitten by the notions of the West. That fellow was named Leonard Slye.

Bob Nobles changed his name to Bob Nolan, and the vocal group became the Sons of the Pioneers. As Bob Nolan he wrote and performed (in a sweet, high tenor) "Tumbling Tumbleweed" and "Cool Water." Amazing.

But maybe not so surprising after all. You grow up in this world of broad silver river and orchards on the hillsides and you end up in the deserts of Arizona and California, and you can think a lot about water. Cool Water.

Leonard Slye? Oh, he changed his name to Roy Rogers.

Amazing.

But none of that meant much to me when I was cycling above the river. I was thinking about the river. It was a transportation system which tied the world together differently in the nineteenth century than it does now. For example, the local farmers took their big barrels of bright red apples down to the nearby wharf — you can see some of the wharves, still there — where the apples were picked up by river-boat (most of them sidewheelers, in fact, and they plied the St. John well into the twentieth century), and taken thence to Saint John, where they were shipped immediately to Boston, New York, London. The river meant that you and your apple were world travellers. Now we pick up a flat electronic image on TV and think we've been some-where. We haven't.

If you drop in to the Eveleigh Hotel, however, right there at the Evandale Ferry on Route 102, you'll see photographs of the old river steamers and pick up a story or two about the days when the Eveleigh Hotel was essentially a riverboat hotel. Or maybe a new story about the scruffy little fellow who turned up one day to rent a cottage and was shortly heard howling like a wolf in the dining room — to the de-light of the children in the room. He was telling them a story, and wolf howls were essential. The little fellow was Farley Mowat.

You can begin this ride at the Eveleigh Hotel, of course, but as it happened I began at Hatfield Point, the little community up the Belleisle Bay. It was a day trip for me. I parked my van beside the Hatfield Point Community Centre — across from which was a large empty common space where some teenaged boys were playing a rousing and vigorous game of football. Not touch football: tackle. No equipment of course except laughter. The grass was thick and soft and they flung one another about with abandon. Their game gradually began to at-tract spectators. It was obviously the kind of place you might stop your car just to watch for a while, with no idea of who was winning, and it was unlikely if anyone, including the players, knew what the score was. One of the specators was a girl who came cantering up on her high-tailed roan. I liked that.

Where to Stay

Oak Point Provincial Park on Route 102 (*not* to be confused with Oak *Bay* Provincial Park, which is some distance away) is 10 km (6 mi) from an entrance to the loop at Evandale ferry. (Those 20 km [12 mi] might be a serious consideration concerning this route; you might want to drive a vehicle to Evandale or Hatfield Point to begin this loop. You might think this is a tough ride.)

But Oak Point Provincial Park promises to have the flush toilets and hot showers which cyclists need, and should be a nice camp-ground. I couldn't inspect it, however, because it is open only from June through September. *Oak Point Provincial Park, Oak Point, New Brunswick E0G 1K0; (506) 468-2266.*

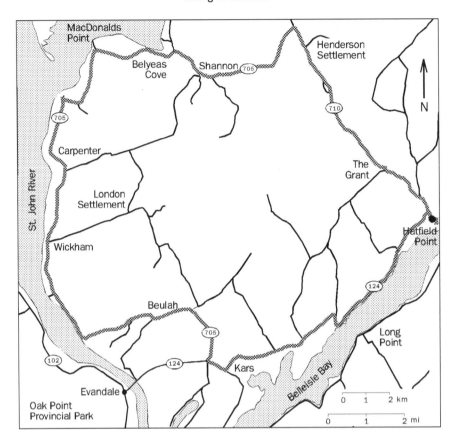

The Eveleigh, which advertises itself as "The Last of the River-boat Hotels," was built in 1889 by John O. VanWart, whose name is still on the window looking out over the river. It offers 10 rooms, 3 motel units and 2 cabins. One of the cabins is equipped for house-keeping. The dining room features seafood casseroles and prime rib, and there is a licensed lounge. *The Eveleigh Hotel, R.R. #1, Evandale, Hampstead, New Brunswick E0G 1Y0; (506) 425-9993 and (506) 425-2591; (800)-561-2828.*

The Ride

This ride is entirely on paved surface, so you can use a ten-speed if you like — but you may want the gears available on a mountain bike. When I started this ride I thought I'd count the times I dropped into granny-gears, but I lost track of the number. I thought the hills might be easier if I cycled clockwise, and that may have been true, though not by much. Even so, the scenery is very beautiful.

I began at Hatfield Point at the Hatfield Point Community Centre on Route 124. Take Route 124 in a westerly direction toward the Evandale ferry. Just before the ferry crossing you will meet Route 705, which goes off to your right in a northerly direction. Turn right and follow Route 705 through the little communities of Wickham and MacDonalds Point. At Belyeas Cove the road itself turns right and northeasterly and you continue on it through Shannon and the forest primeval until you come to the T at Route 710. It is well-marked. Turn right, southeasterly, on Route 710 and return to Hatfield Point.

SUSSEX VALLEY

DISTANCE: 36 km (22 mi)	**OTHER FACTORS:** There are a
TIME: 2 hrs	few short hills which require
DIFFICULTY: Easy to Moderate	low gears.

The Comfort of Cows

A beautiful valley is a terrible attraction. You find yourself above it, and swooping down into it (you feel like a bird — perhaps a swallow), and you think: this is glory. You look around at its pleasant slopes and its contented cows, for whom you are the high point of the present (they have no past), and you think that you could live in harmony with cows. You come upon a village, and you think that a community in harmony with cows and a valley must be a wonderful place to live. You begin to look for signs which might indicate a house for sale or for rent. You think of the sense of shelter which a valley offers — from the winds, the wicked world, change, fads. Vague memories of reading about *Shangri-La* stir back there in your mind before thought; and what was the only place of sanity in Voltaire's *Candide*? *Eldorado*, yes. Where gold was valued as much as butter and no more. You begin to consider metaphysics: a valley is a bowl full of sky; a valley is a cup of God.

You begin — this is becoming dangerous, now — to think of hiding your bike, changing your name, and taking up some quiet occupation like cowherd. You might picture yourself in your new name and old clothes following the hefty ladies out of the field at evening, plop, plop, plop. In your mind you put an idle weed in your mouth; you are ambling; you are becoming dangerously sentimental. A real farmer (wearing a tractor cap, of course) would whoop and holler at this picture you are having of yourself, and you think that you would be wise to keep this to yourself — and anyway, then you remember that there are no cowherds anymore, and when you contemplate the languid girls standing on the hillsides, their big bovine brown eyes on you in unblinking gaze, you remember that what awaits them morning and night is the milking parlour with its efficient machines pumping the milk out of them directly into sealed containers for the milk tanker on its rounds, and you think that perhaps you had better think twice before giving up your name and bicycle. You've been wise.

But aside from that temptation, this ride in Sussex Valley is wonderful, through some beautiful country. It begins at a fine old railway station which is still in occasional use and is therefore spruced up and painted as in days of old. Use the washroom. Grand old place. Reminds a person of the old days. Funny the things that trigger the memory. Fill your water bottle. The station is right in the heart of Sussex — in fact it might be said to have created the heart of Sussex some years ago when railways defined the world. Across from the station is a fine little café where (O wonder of wonders) next to the cash register is a little note advertising bicycle repairs. (No wonder, really. The fellow who operates the café with his wife is the fellow who laid out this route for the Recreation Branch of New Brunswick Tourism.) And in the row of shops on either side of the café you will find an art gallery, a bakery, and a bicycle shop. Sussex, you might conclude, lives well looking backwards.

This consideration might well be seconded by your ride. This route is advertised in a New Brunwick cycling brochure as the Covered Bridge Route, and sure enough, you will cycle through three covered bridges and visit a fourth. At one of them you will glance down and see a gathering of kids fishing there as if in a Norman Rockwell painting, and you might well stop and wonder about a swim. Stick your hand in the water. Think twice. The water is very cold. I've always been dubious about Norman Rockwell anyway.

Where to Stay

If you are camping, you are probably staying at one of the 6 campgrounds at Fundy National Park, and driving (62 km [39 mi]) to the Sussex Railway Station to park your car and lift your bicycles from your rack. *Fundy National Park, P.O. Box 40, Alma, New Brunswick E0A 1B0; (506) 887-2000.*

Accommodation right on the loop can be obtained at the Fairway Motor Inn and Restaurant, which is an unusually well-equipped establishment, right at the junctions of Highways 1 and 2. *Fairway Motor Inn and Restaurant, P.O. Box 1757, Sussex, New Brunswick E0E 1P0; (506) 433-3470.*

Our investigative staff reported (with little ecstasies) that quite superior accommodation can also be found at the three-star establishment of Stark's Hillside Bed and Breakfast, just off Routes 111, 1, and 2. *Stark's Hillside Bed and Breakfast, R.R. #4, Waterford, Sussex, New Brunswick E0E 1P0; (506) 433-3764.*

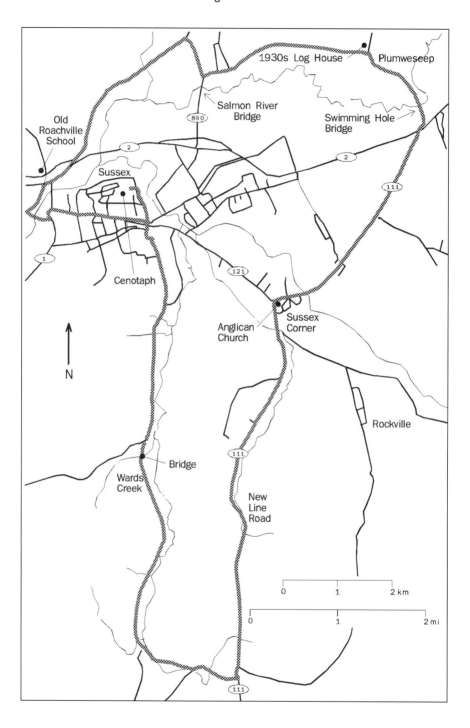

Plumweseep
1930s Log House
Salmon River Bridge
890
Swimming Hole Bridge
Old Roachville School
2
2
111
Sussex
Cenotaph
N
121
Anglican Church
Sussex Corner
1
Rockville
111
Bridge
Wards Creek
New Line Road

0   1   2 km

0   1   2 mi

111

111

The Ride

This route was laid out by Peter Williams, a ten-speeder, and sure enough, your ten-speed can take you everywhere along it just as well as the tough little mountain bike.

Leave the railway station past the cenotaph, cross the tracks, and turn right on Church Avenue. Climb the second-gear hill past the Victorian houses and go straight to the Stop sign. Stop, and continue on, straight. You are on the Ward's Creek Road, although I did not see any signs with that information. You will come to a split in the road. A cemetery is on your left. Bear left and continue straight on past cows and farms to Ward's Creek Bridge. Continue through the covered bridge and straight on until you come to a T. This is Route 111. Turn left and prepare for a glorious vista. There is a long glide down to Sussex Corner. Turn left at the Stop sign, and, in the community of Sussex Corner, right at the Anglican church. You are still on Route 111, although I didn't see any signs to this effect. Winter is hard on signs around here. Ride to the junction with Route 2, the Trans-Canada. You are going to zig right and zag left quickly here; you are aiming for the covered bridge which you can see from your stop at the busy highway. Be careful crossing this dangerous road. There will be evidence of a swimming hole under this bridge.

Continue straight on this road to the community of Plumweseep. You will turn left here at an intersection which is marked by a Gothic outhouse (now in use as a chicken coop) on one corner, and a 1930s log house on the other. This community seems dedicated to auto repair and is surprisingly tidy. Turn left so that the 1930s log house is on your right and cycle onwards. At the next T, you will see (across the road, to your left) yet another covered bridge, this one now in use as a picnic park. You continue the route from the T by turning right and cycling to the next T, where you will turn left. There are a couple of short challenging inclines along this stretch. You will see the town of Sussex off to your left, beyond the meandering stream. You are soon at the back of the Fairway Motel. If you are not staying here, continue on to the next T at Roachville. You can see the Old Roachville School in the distance, but you are turning here well before it, and heading in the direction of Sussex. There is a Stop sign. Stop. Dangerous intersection. Continue straight. You will see a suspension foot bridge to your left. Who could resist? Walk your bike across the suspension bridge (*I* am certainly not going to advise you otherwise) and across the highways in the direction of the McDonald's and Tim Horton's establishments, where you will pick up the main drag in Sussex and follow it as it curves inevitably to the railway station.

BOIESTOWN, LUDLOW and DOAKTOWN

DISTANCE: 48 km (30 mi); 52 km (33 mi) to Red Pines Campground **TIME:** 3 hr 30 min	**DIFFICULTY:** Moderate to Difficult **OTHER FACTORS:** Rough road; mountain bike required.

The Banks of the Miramichi

Songs of lament are common along the banks of the beautiful Miramichi River. This is logging country, and in the nineteenth century many a young man lost his life in this hard business. One was a young fellow named Peter Emberley, who came here from Prince Edward Island, the "garden in the seas," in 1880, and was killed a year later while loading logs. A local singer named John Calhoun told the story:

> *There's danger in the lumber woods*
> *For death lurks sullen there.*
> *And I have fell a victim*
> *Into that monstrous snare.*

You can learn much about the logging industry of the nineteenth century in the Central New Brunswick Woodmen's Museum in Boiestown, which is perhaps the finest museum of its kind you could imagine. (The word *lumberjack*, by the way, is not usually used around here.) Everyone in the community seems to have contributed something to the museum: there is a bunkhouse from Emberley's era, so you can see how he lived in the woods, and a trapper's cabin, and a little logging railway — and even a horse-drawn hearse, and (for a surprise) a Russian samovar and its story. In the museum you can learn about the Great Fire of the Miramichi, which in 1825 killed hundreds and burned the province from the north shore nearly to Fredericton.

The word *Miramichi*, incidentally, is pronounced with the emphasis on the last syllable: Mir-a-ma-**shee**. But don't worry if you cannot pronounce the word correctly right off. Neither can the Queen. (She pronounces it Mir-a-**mit**-chee, but she's the Queen; no one has ever corrected her.)

But if life has always been hard here, and frequently dangerous, it is also graced by unusual natural beauty. The Miramichi River is one of the most beautiful rivers in the world, as well as one of the most famous, especially among salmon anglers. There is the Miramichi Atlantic Salmon Museum in Doaktown, and a famous tackle shop, and a legendary baseball player once had a fishing camp hereabouts, and you'll hear stories of an astronaut's visit — to fish.

This ride takes you up one side of the river, and back down the other. If you are cycling at the right time of the year, you'll see the anglers at their sport, flicking their long lines in lazy S's onto the surface of the water. It's a curiously attractive gesture — as William Butler Yeats, the great Irish poet, noted some time ago about a fly-fisherman in another country. He remembered the fly-fisherman,

> *Climbing up to a place*
> *Where stone is dark under froth,*
> *And the down-turn of his wrist*
> *When the flies drop in the stream*

and concluded that the fly-fisherman deserved commemoration with a "Poem maybe as cold/ And passionate as the dawn."

I took this ride accompanied by my friend Lane MacIntosh, whose pedigree I envy. His father was a professional hockey player; his mother was an opera singer. Lane is now a travel writer and comedian, but when I met him he was a genuine hippie, living in the woods, baking croissants which he sold on Saturday mornings in Fredericton's famous Boyce Market, and reading Thoreau. It is reading Thoreau which qualified him as a genuine hippie. Baking croissants was a respectable means for a fellow living in the woods to make a living.

The ride takes us along the abandoned rail line of the famous Dungarvon Whooper, the little old train that is no more (the last passenger train took this route on January 19, 1961, a day of woe). The train was in turn named after a famous Miramichi story about the cook's apprentice who was murdered in a logging camp. You can still hear his screams on dark nights, whether windy or still.

But it was Lane MacIntosh who first told me the story of the tragedy at the Priceville Bridge. You will ride past the Priceville Bridge. You might even cross it. It feels good to cross a footbridge with a bit of a sway in it. It can give you a thrill. There are few human structures more graceful and more accommodating to the individual human on foot than a footbridge. A footbridge is worth seeking out. A footbridge is delightful probably because of some ancient urge to fly or hang suspended over the rushing waters. But for the five men who tried to cross the old single-span Priceville Bridge on May 10, 1939, it was a foolhardy trip, because their combined weight pulled down the single span into the rushing waters of the springtime-swollen Miramichi, and the water tugged at the bridge and pulled it downstream until one of the cables broke and the bridge snapped back. You can find the story told more fully in *A History of Early Boiestown* by Grace MacMillan Spencer, which you can purchase at the Woodmen's Museum. I did. I recommend it. Of the five men, two survived. One man drowned inches away from being saved. The bridge now has two spans.

There are many, many stories along the Miramichi.

The old railbed here has been maintained by local snowmobilers and off-road vehicle enthusiasts who have established friendly relations with adjacent landowners and householders. The project has been one of entirely local initiative. Cyclists owe all of these people a vote of thanks — so say thank you if you get the opportunity.

Where to Stay

There is an excellent campground, the Red Pines Park, just across from the Central New Brunswick Woodmen's Museum, operated by the community in the name of the museum. It features shade, hot showers and flush toilets, and has 63 sites, 40 of them serviced. *Red Pines Park, P.O. Box 7, Boiestown, New Brunswick E0H 1A0; (506) 369-2393.*

Just north of Boiestown, on the Porter Cove Road, just across the bridge off Route 8, in the community of Ludlow, is Pond's Chalet Resort — which caters usually to fly-fishermen who like rustic comfort. There is a large sign to direct you on Route 8. Pond's Resort has 45 units, many of them separate chalets, and several of them with wood stoves and Hudson's Bay blankets. All the buildings are nestled under tall pines alongside the river. You have the feeling that you are properly in the North Woods. The restaurant is exceptionally good and, as you might expect, features salmon and large portions of everything. Lane and I spent a lazy afternoon there, eating and eating more, after our ride. *Pond's Chalet Resort, Porter Cove Road, Ludlow, New Brunswick E0C 1N0; (506) 369-2612.*

The Ride

You will need a mountain bike for this ride.

If you are staying at the Red Pines Campground you will cycle (very carefully) about 4 km (2.5 mi) on Route 8 to Porter's Cove Road.

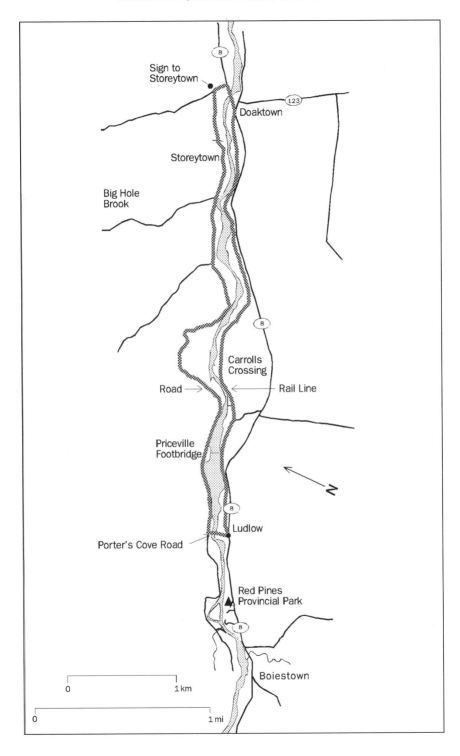

Sign to
Storeytown

Doaktown

Storeytown

Big Hole
Brook

Carrolls
Crossing

Road → ← Rail Line

Priceville
Footbridge

Ludlow

Porter's Cove Road

Red Pines
Provincial Park

Boiestown

0   1 km

0   1 mi

The old railbed is no more than 50 m (50 yds) from Route 8. There you "put in" (the canoe term seems apt in these parts). You will find the occasional leftover railway tie or little washout to keep you alert, but the surface is generally firm and smooth. Ride the old railbed in a northeasterly direction through the canopy of trees above the river for about 6 km (4 mi) to the place where you will spot the Priceville Bridge. Continue on until you find yourself in a bit of a wrinkle at Carrolls Crossing, where the railbed seems to disappear. You will be on a road by a fenced field for perhaps 1 km (.5 mi) or so, but while you are climbing a moderately difficult hill, you will spot the railbed again halfway up the hill, to your left. Continue on the old railbed until you end up in a barnyard outside the village of Doaktown. From here you will ride on the broad paved shoulder of Route 8 through Doaktown. *If you need food or drink, get it here: there will be no other chance.* On the other side of town — perhaps 100 m (100 yds) beyond the Doaktown Post Office — you will see the railbed curving off to your left. Follow it and walk your bicycle across the old rail bridge and, at the northern end of the bridge, take the road uphill to your right, granny-gears welcome, and ride parallel to Route 8 to the sign which directs travellers to Storeytown. Turn left, westerly, on that road. It is chipseal as far as the gathering of houses called Storey-town (the mailboxes explain the name) and thereafter dirt and gravel for some distance. This is logging country on this side of the river, and you will be glad of your granny-gears and your fat tires. At last you will come to a steep rough downhill — hang onto your brakes — and you'll find yourself at Priceville, the other side of the swinging bridge. Now the road is paved. Continue on straight (westerly), perhaps stopping at the roadside spring to fill your water bottles, to the sign directing you to Route 8. This is Porter's Cove Road. If you are staying at Pond's Resort, you will find it just before the bridge. If you are staying at the Red Pines Campground, you have another 4 km (2.5 mi) to go.

CAMPBELLTON

Ride One	Ride Two
DISTANCE: 27 km (17 mi) Sugarloaf to Sugarloaf; 37 km (23 mi) Campbellton to Campbellton	**DISTANCE:** 44 km (27 mi) Sugarloaf to Sugarloaf; 54 km (34 mi) Campbellton to Campbellton
TIME: 1 hr 30 min or 2 hrs	**TIME:** 3 hrs
DIFFICULTY: Easy	**DIFFICULTY:** Difficult
	OTHER FACTORS: Long steep hills

Valleys of Passion

Are you ready for the shadows of the glen?

This ride takes you through the village of Val d'Amour — there's no need to translate that, is there? — past some of the detritus of the twentieth century (you'll see what I mean when you get there), and into the deep valley between close hills where the shadows are dark green and the mist rises like smoke. It is not difficult to imagine indistinct figures concealed in the trees. The valley is called Glencoe, and it commemorates (in a way) the massacre of the MacDonalds by the Campbells (led by John Campbell of Breadalbane) at Glencoe in Argyll in Scotland on February 13, 1692. History in the Maritimes is tucked into the damnedest places. It always surprises you. Is it ironic — and was it considered fitting — that the nearby town is named Campbellton?

Where to Stay

Sugarloaf Provincial Park, on Route 270, just off the major highway, Route 11, not only provides a campground with flush toilets and hot showers, but in addition boasts tennis courts and hiking trails, and a canteen (snack bar) with aspects of a nightclub, and a tourist information centre. *Sugarloaf Provincial Park, C.P. 639, Campbellton, New Brunswick E3N 3H1; (506) 753-7706.*

The Sanfar Cottages, beside the Restigouche River on Route 134 between Tide Head and Atholville, New Brunswick, is right on the loop and offers clean, comfortable and reasonably priced cottage accommodations with a continental breakfast included in the tariff.

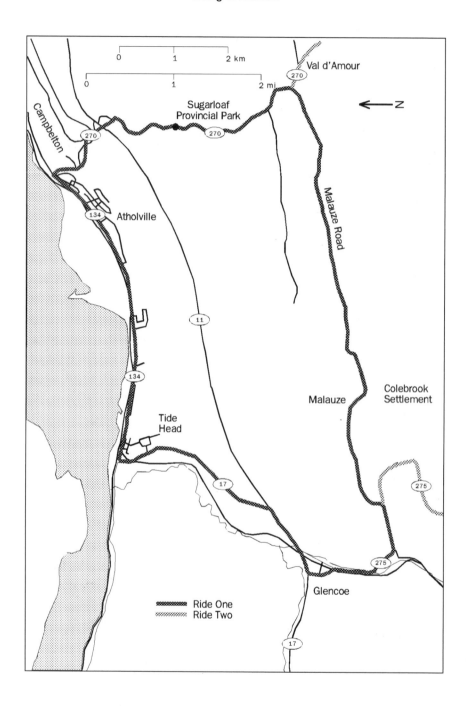

Service is bilingual English and French. A licensed dining room, the Country Kettle, is part of the establishment, so evening meals are available. I stopped here to visit and thought it an unusually attractive place for cyclists. *Sanfar Cottages and Country Kettle, Restigouche Drive, Tide Head, Campbellton, New Brunswick E0K 1K0; (506) 753-4287.*

The Aylesford Inn Bed and Breakfast is an operatic (you'll see what I mean if you stop here) four-star bilingual Heritage Inn in Campbellton. The staff is accustomed to cyclists and can direct you to a nearby bicycle mechanic if repairs to your cycle are necessary. The ambience is Victorian — and an afternoon tea is served on Monday, Wednesday and Friday. *Aylesford Inn, 8 McMillan Avenue, Campbellton, New Brunswick E3N 1E9; (506) 759-7672.*

Ride One

This ride is easy and comparatively short if you are cycling from Sugarloaf Provincial Park; longer if you are cycling out from Campbellton. It is suitable for all sorts of bicycles, although there is a short stretch of gravel on the Malauze Road which might cause difficulty for ten-speed bikes.

The ride begins at Sugarloaf Provincial Park. Come out of the park and turn left and ride in a southerly direction on Route 270 alongside the brook which leads you to the village of Val d'Amour. It is a curious little village which you might want to explore, but the ride takes a right turn westerly on the Malauze Road (marked) just before the village of Val d'Amour. The Malauze Road suggests in different ways that life can be hard. A gravel pit suggests that the mountains hereabouts are glacial deposit, and that the gravel trucks just back up to the mountain and fill up with part of it. Not surprisingly, there is a short stretch (no more than 2 km [1 mi]) of gravel. The Malauze Road comes to a T with Route 275. Turn right, northerly, on Route 275 through the shadows of Glencoe, past the terrible harvest of wrecked cars which have come from elsewhere to die, to the T at Route 17. Turn right, easterly, and follow Route 17 to the huge overhead sign which points you left to Tide Head and Atholville and Route 134. Go there. You are on the connecting road to Route 134. At the T in Tide Head turn right, easterly, and ride Route 134 through Tide Head past (or to) the Sanfar Cottages to the mill town of Atholville, where you will turn right, southerly, on Route 270 to Sugarloaf Provincial Park. Follow the signs to Sugarloaf.

If you are staying in Campbellton (at the Aylesford Inn, for example), you will have used Route 134 to get to this loop and return from it. You will add another 5 km + 5 km going and coming to your total distance.

Ride Two

Peter Williams, of Velo New Brunswick, produced a cycling guide for Tourism New Brunswick which uses a very similar route. If you want to try Peter's route, instead of turning on the Malauze Road at Val d'Amour, continue on Route 270 up to the junction with Route 275. Then turn right, westerly, on Route 275, which crosses the hilltops through Saint-Arthur and curves downhill and northerly through Glencoe to Tide Head. Pavement all the way.

Peter notes that this route is for "experienced cyclists . . . you should have strong legs." Believe him. He's absolutely right. It is a 44 km (27 mi) route with some mean, mean hills.

MAISONNETTE, CARAQUET and LE VILLAGE HISTORIQUE ACADIEN

DISTANCE: 31 km (19 mi) **TIME:** 1 hr 30 min	**DIFFICULTY:** Easy to Moderate, depending on . . . **OTHER FACTORS:** The wind off the sea.

The Slant of Trees

There is a deal of sea air in Maisonnette. Suck it in. It's what you came here for, isn't it? Unless you are here for the history, which is considerable: the ride begins in the parking lot of the Acadian Village, which takes you back a century or more to a time when the French-speaking people who fled here in 1755 re-established their community: the museum depicts their lives from 1780 to 1890. I was particularly interested in the growing, drying and harvesting of marsh hay. It's an ingenious agricultural practice, and any demonstration of ingenuity, to my way of thinking, is rewarding in itself.

This ride is government-authorized. I've taken it from one of Peter Williams's brochures for Tourism New Brunswick. It's a very pleasant ride, especially if you like sea air. I am sucking it in in the little picnic park with swimming beach at Maisonnette, where the water is reputedly unusually warm. I'm not chancing the water today: the air is sufficiently bracing and in a good stiff breeze. From the slant of the trees it is evident that this is not the first day for a good stiff breeze.

Where to Stay

The Caraquet Provincial Park is located on Highway 11, on the water at Caraquet. It has flush toilets and hot showers and a nice little beach. You will find here, as elsewhere in the Acadian Peninsula, that whatever French you possess will be useful. *Carquet Provincial Park, Ste-Anne-du-Bocage, Caraquet, New Brunswick E0B 1K0; (506) 727-3474.*

Our investigative staff reports that a good, popular hostelry in Caraquet is the Hotel Paulin, which is known locally as Chez Nous Nous. *Hotel Paulin, 143 Blvd St-Pierre Ouest, Caraquet, New Brunswick E0B 1K0; (506) 727-9981.*

The Ride

Leave the parking lot of the Acadian Museum, turn left on Highway 11 and ride approximately 2 km (1.25 mi) north to the junction with Route 303, to your right. Turn right, northeasterly, on Route 303 and ride to and through the pleasant village (just the right size for itself) of Maisonnette to the picnic park, where you will find toilets and sinks and picnic shelters.

Leaving the park, ride back through Maisonnette, southwesterly, to the road marked Anse Bleu just on the southwest edge of the village. In fact, you may have to interpret the sign somewhat; only half of it was there the day I was there. But turn right in the direction of Anse Bleu (you cannot really go wrong), and ride to the north coast of this peninsula, where you will turn left on Route 320 (I do not recall seeing a sign) and ride along the north coast, which is called Anse Bleu, back to Highway 11. Lots of good bracing sea air through Anse Bleu, much of it directly in my face. I returned the healthier for it. Turn left on Highway 11 in a southerly direction back to the parking lot of the Acadian Village.

MAISONNETTE, CARAQUET and LE VILLAGE HISTORIQUE ACADIEN

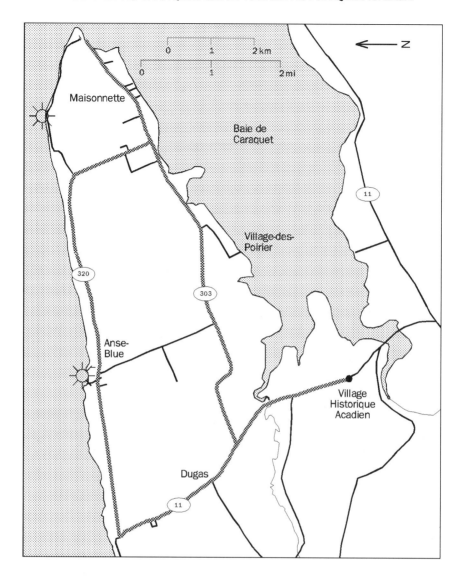

LAMÈQUE

DISTANCE: 49 km (30 mi) around the island of Lamèque. Diversion to Miscou Lighthouse is additional 36 km (22 mi).	**TIME:** 2 hrs 30 min **DIFFICULTY:** Moderate **OTHER FACTORS:** Wind off the sea.

Whizzer

Welcome to Lamèque. It's a lovely island off the northeast coast of New Brunswick which is full of surprises — like baroque music at the end of July, performed on period instruments at the church of Ste-Cécile, which is right on Route 113 and is part of the loop around the island which you will ride. The International Baroque Music Festival brings instrumental groups to Lamèque from all over the world to perform the delights of seventeenth and eighteenth century music. Does the Bach family charm you? The red-headed Vivaldi, who composed for his all-girl orchestra? You can hear the charming tones of another era which resonate in your soul.

In a structure of another era. The church of Ste-Cécile dominates the landscape. There are at least two others which do, as well. They were all built at the turn of this century, when the spiritual life of the Roman Catholic Church dwarfed the everyday concerns of getting by and hauling a living from the sea. The churches are ten times the height of any other buildings on the island.

There was even perhaps—the issue isn't quite settled yet — a religious miracle on Lamèque. André Chiasson was born here in 1939 and at seven months old suffered from hydrocephalus. His mother asked the spirit of a nun of the order of the Sisters of Jesus and Mary in Quebec City, Dina Belanger (who had died in 1929), to assist the infant, and on the ninth day of the mother's vigil, the child began to recover. In 1993 André Chiasson journeyed to Rome to participate in ceremonies beatifying Dina Belanger, who needs one more miracle to qualify for sainthood. Chiasson says it is sometimes awkward being the recipient of an official miracle: people expect you to pass the magic on.

For me, there was another kind of relic of great importance. I was zipping down Route 305 near the end of the loop when I spotted, off to the right, on display among other interesting artifacts in a fellow's own private exhibition, a Whizzer Motorbike.

What was a Whizzer? It was a belt-driven motorbike which was very popular when I was a youth. The first Whizzers were in fact motors with belt-drives attached to the heavy, balloon-tired Schwinns some of us rode back then. The Whizzer motor and belt-drive converted the bicycle into a motorbike.

But it was soon evident that the Whizzer motor, however light, was nonetheless too heavy even for the the sturdy Schwinn, and quickly heavier bicycles were built with stronger frames, heavier rims, and thicker spokes especially to take the Whizzer motor. I had one of these for a time. It could hit 60 mph on the highway easy. It terrified even me, and I was sixteen and of course thought myself immortal, as one does at sixteen. Perhaps the Whizzer made me question my mortality, and a good thing, too.

In any event, the adapted bike version of the Whizzer soon disappeared, to be replaced by something very beautiful: a little belt-driven motorcycle designed around the Whizzer motor. One of my best friends had one. I envied him. It was a forest green; it was gorgeous. He sometimes let me ride pillion. I wanted one.

And never got one. The Whizzer on display in Lamèque is old and battered and patched and painted red and silver — but it is the same creature. Of course you should stop to view it. Perhaps the creator of the exhibition will come out to talk to you as he came out to talk to me. He had less English than I had French and I have almost no French. We gazed at the wonderful machine and said the word *Whizzer* a great deal. We enjoyed ourselves immensely. The entire exhibit was set off with a black chain of huge links which drooped from post to post. He was immensely proud of it. It was made entirely of bottle-caps. It was wonderful.

The first language of Lamèque (the island and the major village have the same name) is French, but your English will do.

Not too far past the wonderful Whizzer exhibit is another relic of the fifties: a drive-in movie. It proclaims itself in large letters: VÉNUS CINÉPARC. Was there ever elsewhere such poetic honesty as this? This *is* an unusual place. Do you remember? The windows would fog even on a balmy night. You probably don't remember. You may never have known. Pity. Church was awkward the next day.

Where to Stay

There is a municipal campground 5 km (3 mi) from the village of Lamèque on Route 113. I began my ride from there. It is a shaded, pleasant, old-fashioned campground with the requisite hot showers and flush toilets and good tenting sites. *Camping Municipal, Ville de Lamèque, C.P. 58, Lamèque, New Brunswick E0B 1V0; (506) 344-8416.*

Highly recommended, and a favourite with those who attend the Baroque Music Festival, is La Ferme Larocque bed and breakfast, where the lobster omelette is said to resonate in the soul like Bach. Word has gotten round, of course, so you would be wise to reserve — and reserve early. *La Ferme Larocque (Anaclet Larocque), 169 rue du Pêcher, C.P. 28, Lamèque, New Brunswick E0B 1V0; (506) 344-8860.*

The Ride

All of this ride is on paved road, so a ten-speed road bike can be used, although a mountain bike or hybrid is recommended (some of these are secondary roads, far from the centres of government influence), and if you decide to detour north to the tip of Miscou Island, a mountain bike will be required.

I cycled out from the Campground Municipal, which is 5 km (3 mi) north of the village of Lamèque, on Route 113 north to the departure point of the Miscou Island ferry. It was a free five-minute ferry ride. However, a bridge was being built at the time — which should be completed by the time you are there, depending on provincial finances and political vagaries

If you decide to venture out to Miscou Island Lighthouse (in continuous service since 1856), you will detour to the tune of 18 km there and 18 km back — 36 km (22 mi). I drove a motor vehicle there and back, but decided not to cycle it.

Just past the ferry (or bridge) the road turns back on itself (south) and seems bent on returning to the village of Lamèque. This is in fact the most direct route from the ferry (or bridge) to Lamèque, and can be busy with traffic in a hurry in moments. Continue in a southerly direction on this road until you come to the clearly marked Chemin Couteau. Turn left. It is almost a hairpin turn and takes you back in a northeasterly direction past peat fields and tiny communities to the junction with Route 305. The sign here points forward to Pigeon Hill, but you ignore Pigeon Hill and turn right (southerly) toward Ste-Marie-St-Raphael, which is on the southeastern shore of the island of Lamèque. You will be greeted on the outskirts of the community by a big sign announcing the name of the community, Ste-Marie-St-Raphael, and a golf-driving range. Continue into the community until you come to the church. You can't miss the church. At the crossroads near the church is the Caisse Populaire (on one corner) and the post office, in one part of the community hall, on the other. Now the

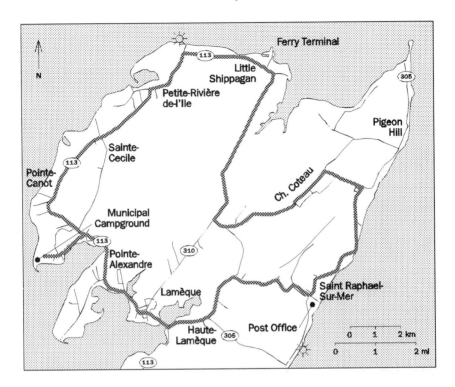

name of the village seems to have changed to St-Raphael-Sur-Mer. Turn right (westerly) on rue Parc at the Caisse Populaire. Follow rue Parc for perhaps 1 km (1000 yards) to rue St Raphael Ouest. It is marked. Turn left. Follow the twisted, populated road through the early years of this century to the T. Turn left at the T. It will take you south to Route 305. Turn right on Route 305 and soon you will see the Whizzer motorbike on your right and the Vénus Cinéparc on your left. At the junction with Route 113, turn right, cross the bridge, and you are in the village of Lamèque. Follow 113 through the village and back to the Campground Municipal.

KOUCHIBOUGUAC

DISTANCE: 25 km (15 mi) **DIFFICULTY:** Very Easy
TIME: 1 hr

Fetching Shorts

I was standing in line to go to a movie (probably something arty by Clint Eastwood) when I happened to mention to my companion, Ms. Luxe, that I was getting flabby. Maybe she offered to buy the popcorn? "Butter?" she asked.

I said, "I'd better go on a diet."

The guy behind me interrupted. "*Girls* go on diets," he said, "*Guys* get in shape."

I had not heretofore recognized the distinction.

But say that you fit into one category or the other and find yourself sitting before the flickering blue image of the TV screen late into the night trying to commit suicide by potato chip by potato chip by potato chip by potato chip, and it occurs to you that it might be a good idea to get a bicycle. Yes, a bicycle might be interesting: out in the open air, singing along on the tires — why, you can see yourself becoming lean and perky. And cycling shorts are . . . well . . . *fetching*.

You say to your companion, "Let's go on a bicycling holiday."

Your companion replies, with an air of being more reasonable and understanding than usual: "We'll die."

"No, no, no," you say. "We'll begin sensibly and work up to the cycling shorts."

"Cycling shorts? What are you talking about?"

"We'll begin with some easy rides — and then gradually expand our horizons. Yeah — we'll expand our horizons." (Sounds nice, doesn't it?)

"OK," says the understanding companion, "but where shall we start?"

"Kouchibouguac National Park in New Brunswick," you say.

Your companion is taken somewhat aback. "Why do you say Kouchibouguac National Park?"

"Because," you say triumphantly, "I can pronounce it. I have read Thompson's book, and he says it is a good place to start."

"All right, then," says your companion, idly smashing the television set in passing *en route* to pack for the trip, "but it had better not be dangerous."

Cycling is about as safe as it can be at Kouchibouguac National Park, which is pronounced Coo-joo-boo-**quack** Nash-un-al Prk. Kouchibouguac National Park is located off Highway 11 and Route 134 about midway between Moncton and Chatham on the eastern coast of New Brunswick. What you will find there are 25 km (15 mi) of nicely groomed, well-packed gravel bicycle roadways. They are designed especially for you and your bicycle. You can even rent a bicycle if you do not happen to have one. And if you are very, very new to cycling, and unsure of your balance, you can fall off your bicycle and you will bounce into the soft grass. It is not absolutely guaranteed that you will not get hurt, but it is safe to say that you will not be killed. You might be gravel-burned, scraped, sprained and twisted, but nothing worse is likely.

This interest in cycling in national parks is comparatively recent, and may be due (in part) to the success of cycling activities on Mount Desert Island in Acadia National Park at Bar Harbor, Maine, where the Rockefeller estate left forty-five miles of nicely groomed gravel carriage trails to the nation. The paths, which had been engineered to convey the hefty wealthy by horse-drawn carriage through the joys of nature, turned out to be just wonderful for mountain bikes.

"When do we get the cycling shorts?"

"Later."

While you are at Kouchibouguac National Park you can go for a swim in the Lagune de Saint Louis, or in the vastness of the ocean beyond the sandbar. There is a bridge to the sandbar. You can go for nature walks. A boardwalk has been constructed out into the marshes so you can see the flora and (perhaps) the fauna without getting your feet wet.

There is even a restaurant — *Bon Accueil* — which is notable for its cheerful atmosphere, good fish, and absence of French fries. Good home cooking.

I went on a diet; I got out my bicycle; I got in shape.

Where to Stay

You will be camping.

However, you have a choice of two kinds of camping.

You can camp at the major campground with amenities like flush toilets and hot showers handy at the South Kouchibouguac Campground. I camped here with my van. However, there are *no* sites with

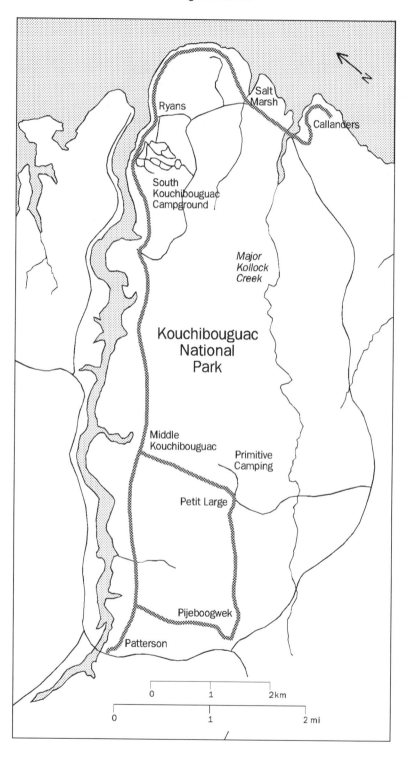

electricity or water anywhere in the park. It is a park designed to encourage tenting. Or you can walk or cycle into the primitive campground at Petit-Large, where you will find pit toilets and well water. You are advised to get to the park early. All campsites are allotted on a first-come first-served basis, and the park is very popular at high season. The park is open for camping from May through October. *Kouchibouguac National Park, Kouchibouguac, New Brunswick E0A 2A0; (506) 876-2443 or (506) 876-4205.*

The Ride

You will be given a map when you enter the park. The map will have bicycle paths marked on it. If you are camping in comparative comfort at South Kouchibouguac Campground, you will leave the camp and cycle westerly (ignoring the first possible turn) to a place called Patterson and turn left and southerly there and cycle to Pijeboogwek, where the trail turns easterly to Petit-Large, where a little branch trail takes you to the primitive campground. Back on the main trail you will find it takes you in a northerly direction back to the trail you began on. Turn right, easterly, and cycle past the South Kouchibouguac Campground and follow the trail along the lagoons past Ryans (bicycle rentals here) to the salt marsh. Here, if you like, you park and lock your bike and take the boardwalk out into the marsh. Return, cycle to a place called Callanders — and return back the way you came.

It is a short, easy ride. More bicycle paths were being constructed when I was at Kouchibouguac, however, so longer rides may now be possible.

PRINCE EDWARD ISLAND

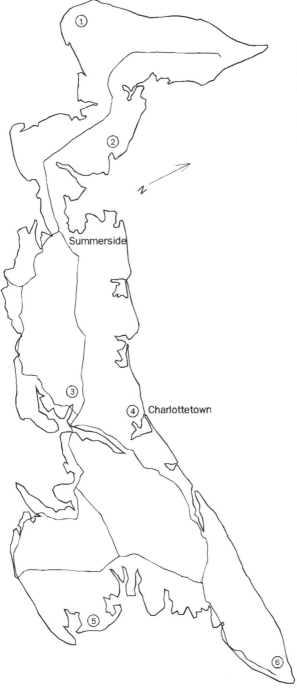

1. West Point
2. Tyne Valley
3. Charlottetown
4. Stanhope and Dalvay
5. Panmure Island
6. Elmira

WEST POINT

DISTANCE: 47 km (30 mi)	**DIFFICULTY:** Easy to Moderate
TIME: 2 hrs 30 min	**OTHER FACTORS:** Wind

Time Travel

This ride will take you alongside the grey-blue sea of the Northumberland Strait and then inland to 1951. Yep. 1951. Time travel.

Which may turn out to be a mixed blessing. Nostalgia is dangerous; the past is dangerous — and very seductive. And there is no denying that this a very pleasant ride. I enjoyed it immensely. I began to think about it with the word *perfect* in mind.

The sea, of course, is a comfort because of its size and eternity. It is always there, good and bad, calm or stormy, slopping about against the land, level, defining a horizon. You know where you are when you can see the horizon.

And then, turning inland through the luxurious green potato fields in the red earth of Prince Edward Island, you have similar feelings that life is good, stable and certain. These are very prosperous farms — and what is as comforting as a prosperous farm? In the fifties families used to drive out into the country in sedate sedans to admire prosperous farms. My family did that. My father thought there was nothing so *satisfactory* as a prosperous farm.

Here we see rows of potato plants stretching in perfectly straight lines to the vanishing point. The houses are solid, tidy, comfortable; their lawns are impressive — not only mowed, but barbered. And suddenly there are two girls of fifteen in a driveway trying out dance steps. No, cheerleading routines. No, majorette moves. Probably majorette moves; the West Point Majorettes are locally famous. The girls stop when they notice me noticing them. But this ride does seem to be a pleasant trip to a pleasanter time. 1951 was a good year. I was there. Not a perfect year, of course. I was there.

It was the year of the conflict in Korea which became what was called a *police action*. Nothing so crude as a *war*. It was an era of delicate language. It was the year when the Rosenbergs were sentenced to death in the U.S. for stealing ideas which inevitably all sorts of other people came up with entirely on their own. There was a peculiar belief — then — that knowledge was a secret you could keep. The deaths of the Rosenbergs were not only cruel, but pointless, futile, ridiculous, embarrassing. They were never talked about much, even then, and certainly not later. We preferred the fifties of the TV series *Happy Days* and the comic strip *Archie and His Friends*. The Sock-Hop. The Malt Shop. The Proms. My high school prom featured a lighthouse in the centre of the school gym; the theme was taken from the popular song, "Harbor Lights."

1951 was also the year that Holden Caulfield popped out of J.D. Salinger's *Catcher in the Rye* to see phoniness in everyone but himself and began his career as a role model for generations of self-righteous teenagers. 1951 was not perhaps a great year.

But, as years go, not bad, if we compare it to some others. When I reach the little town of O'Leary, Prince Edward Island, I see the sign which says *Incorporated 1951*, and in moments I have the notion that nothing has changed since. Why, there's a dime store (now called a *variety store*, of course), and a hardware store, and guys hanging out around the gas station (*filling station, service station, car care centre*), sitting in their cars, windows rolled down, elbows out, looking like three different versions of James Dean, with packs of cigarettes rolled up in their T-shirt sleeves. Well, maybe not the cigarettes. I remember those guys; I was one of them. When you're one of them you know every inch of country road for miles around and where every cheerleader or majorette is practising her steps.

Come to think of it, there are many restored fifties cars in Prince Edward Island. You see them everywhere.

Moreover, there's a charming (yes, that's the word for it) railway station in O'Leary. Of course, there are no trains anymore, haven't been any trains for years. But the station remains, and it contains a beauty shop and a young lawyer's office. He and I talk bicycling for a while. He says it's a car culture around here and nods at the James Deans in their cars at the car care centre. And there used to be a Railway Café in the charming little station, but it couldn't make a go of it.

But outside the post office on the main drag the local doctor is greeting his patients by their first names — he was there at the births of maybe half of them — and they hang around to josh him for a few moments.

No, this is not a bad life. It is tempting to stay here forever, isn't it? Why not live in 1951? Why *should* we always rush after the next thing? There was nothing *wrong*, was there, with Dick & Jane & Spot & Puff? And Dad going to work and Mom the Queen of the House? Can you honestly say that was *bad*? Well . . . maybe not *great*, but *bad*?

Anyway, the ride takes you away from 1951 and back toward the timeless sea, and the campground and lighthouse at West Point. Here the perspective is longer, unsheltered, eternal.

Where to Stay

You have a choice of wonderful accomodations at West Point. The Cedar Dunes Provincial Park (which has miles of sandy beach and dunes) offers electrical hook-ups and water, and hot showers, flush toilets and laundry facilities. You can't beat that — except with this: also available are rental bicycles, including a *tandem*. Wonderful, especially if there's someone with you, as there was not with me when I was there. The park is on Route 14, 24 km (15 mi) from O'Leary. It is open from late June through early September. Reservations accepted after April 1. *Cedar Dunes Provincial Park, Department of Tourism and Parks, Parks Division West, Woodstock, R.R. #3, O'Leary, Prince Edward Island C0B 1V0; (902) 859-2711; (winter) (902) 859-2448.*

If there's someone with you, you might want to consider very seriously the adjacent West Point Lighthouse Inn. Yes, a working lighthouse, eighty-five feet tall, gazing out across the water to New Brunswick. You can walk to the West Point Lighthouse Inn from the Cedar Dunes Provincial Park, and yes, you can have breakfast, lunch and an evening meal there, and yes, it is licensed. Even better, there are 9 rooms to be rented in the West Point Lighthouse Inn, all with private baths, and 2 with whirlpool baths. Better still, 2 of the bedrooms are in the lighthouse itself, and one of them has a *canopy bed* and the other has a *fainting couch*. Are you on your honeymoon? Here you can honeymoon beside the eternal sea — and cycle back to 1951. The inn is open from mid-May through late September. *West Point Lighthouse Inn, West Point, R.R. #2, O'Leary, Prince Edward Island C0B 1V0; (902) 859-3605, (winter) (902) 859-3117.*

The Ride

This ride is suitable for all kinds of bicycles, although the Kennedy Road is a dirt road, and a mountain bike would be best.

The ride begins at either the Cedar Dunes Provincial Campground or the West Point Lighthouse Inn: they are side by side and share the same road out to Route 14, where you turn left (northwesterly) and continue on Route 14 beside the sea until you come to Route 142 at West Cape. Turn right (northeasterly) on Route 142 and ride straight to O'Leary. In O'Leary you will turn right (southeasterly) at the United Church. You might see this road identified as the Barclay Road and notice that you

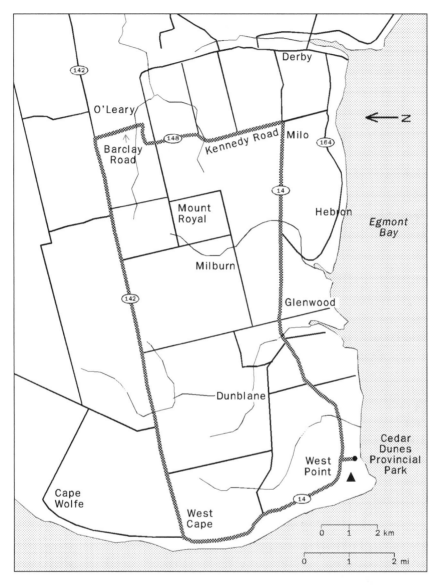

are passing the buildings identified as West Prince Regional Services. You are in fact on Route 148, but I found no signs with numbers to indicate this. When you come to a T, turn right (southwesterly) and in perhaps a kilometre or so, turn left (southeasterly) on the Kennedy Road. There is a sign identifying the Kennedy Road, which is a dirt road. Ride the Kennedy Road to Milo, where you see the little red schoolhouse at the junction with Route 14. Turn right (southwesterly) on Route 14 to both the Cedar Dunes Provincial Park and the West Point Lighthouse Inn.

TYNE VALLEY

DISTANCE: 39 km (24 mi) to the provincial park; 37 km (23 mi) if you are staying in Tyne Valley. **TIME:** 2 hrs 30 min	**DIFFICULTY:** Moderate **OTHER FACTORS:** Heavy traffic on Route 2. A mountain bike is recommended for use on the gravel shoulder.

Questions of Value

Have you noticed (I am sure you have) how often the classic double-dip ice cream cone presents you with the classic dilemma of competing values? Here you are, say, at the front of the line at the Richmond Dairy Bar in Richmond, Prince Edward Island. You are midway through your ride and you have stopped for sustenance. It is a lovely summer day — the first in some time, after a disagreeably wet week — and everyone and his dog and his mother-in-law are on the road seeking sunshine and taking a break from one another in the classic manner by "stopping for an ice cream cone." You, however, are on your own. Your only companion is your faithful bicycle. You have ordered, and just received, a bottle of orange juice and a classic strawberry double-dip ice cream. You are wearing cycling gloves. You receive some change. You have two hands and need three. You put a two-dollar bill in your mouth and turn away from the counter. You look like an idiot, eating money. Nobody notices: everybody and his dog and his mother-in-law and kids are in deep and lively discussion about who wants what and what they may, or may not, have. Somebody wails, "I want fries!" You wait to hear the sound of swift retribution, but there is none. People are looking at you with a two-dollar bill in your mouth and an apologetic expression on your face as you hasten toward some level surface to set something down so you can deal with life because already the ice cream — oh, this is a *most - generous* strawberry double-dip ice cream cone — is beginning to melt. The thought of a blob falling off the edge and onto your hand and thence to the dirt below is grievous. There is no level surface to be found. You want to whimper, but it is not done, and you hasten around the corner to ah! a table. Put down the orange juice. Attack the strawberry double-dip ice cream cone. Remember to remove the two-dollar bill from your mouth. Oh, the ice cream is good! Triumph, victory, and just in time!

Well, not quite. You lost a blob there.

Never mind. It is a lovely day and this is Prince Edward Island, the Garden of the Gulf, as it likes to be known, and you have been cycling through the pastoral delights of tidy fields and prosperous farms. The fact is, the word *farm* does not apply easily (in my lexicon, anyhow) to the pastoral ambitions of this part of the island. The word *estates* comes to mind. Lawns — perfect shapes of perfect green — and sudden splashes of wild colour: purple lupins dashing along the roadside. And at Grand River a blue heron takes offence at my notice and heaves himself into slow flight, like a profundity just beyond grasp.

This ride is focused on the village of Tyne Valley, which is a community just big enough to have one of anything you might need — including a small hospital at the top of a short low-gear hill — and a dam and waterfall in the village centre where you can contemplate the beauty of light through falling water. A painter friend of mine says that this light is similar to the light which is caught in glass — which is why he thinks that the chaps who sold Manhattan Island for twenty-four glass beads got the better of the deal. It's a question of what you value, isn't it? I think he's right.

Where to Stay

Green Park Provincial Park is at Port Hill, 6 km (4 mi) east of the village of Tyne Valley on Route 12. It has everything you might think you want, including hot showers and flush toilets — and a beach and a shipbuilding display centre and a beautiful old house. It's open from late June through early September. Reservations are accepted after April 1. *Green Park Provincial Park, Department of Tourism and Parks, Parks Division West, Woodstock, R.R. #3, O'Leary, Prince Edward Island C0B 1V0; (902) 831-2370; (winter) (902) 859-2448*

On my trip to this area I camped at Green Park Provincial Park, but, cycling through the village of Tyne Valley, I stopped to visit at the West Island Inn, which struck me as a cheerful, attractive hostelry, full of antiques and amenable to vacationing cyclists. It is just off Route 12 in the centre of the village. It has 5 rooms with private baths, and a light supper is available on request. Open from May 15 through October 15. *West Island Inn, Box 24, Tyne Valley, Prince Edward Island C0B 2C0; (902) 831-2495.*

The Ride

This loop is suitable for all kinds of bicycles, but a mountain bike will be safer along the short section of heavily travelled Route 2. With a mountain bike you can ride on the wide, firm, gravelled shoulder.

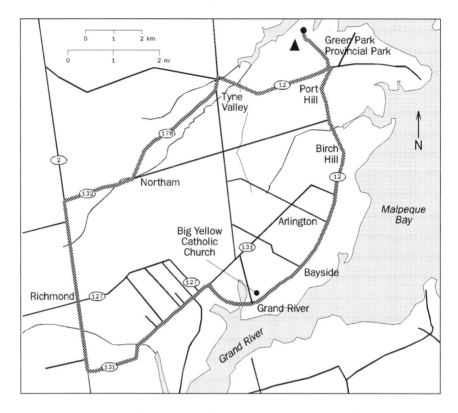

From Green Park Provincial Park you ride about 2 km (1 mi) to Route 12, and take Route 12 (ignoring all other possibilities) along the west coast of Malpeque Bay to Grand River, where you will see the very large, very yellow St. Patrick's Roman Catholic Church, and just beyond it a small bridge. Immediately after the bridge the road is joined by Route 131, and you ride Route 12 and Route 131 together until the next intersection, which is within 2 km (1 mi). When I was here a useful sign was down and lying in the grass; when you are here it should be upright again. The intersection is with Route 127. Cross Route 127 and continue straight on Route 131 south to Route 2. Turn right on Route 2 and ride on the gravelled shoulder through Richmond — stopping at the Richmond Dairy Bar for ice cream and contemplation of values — to Route 132. Pay attention to these digits. Turn right on Route 132 (northeasterly) to Route 178. You will see evidence here of the old rail-line which has not yet been turned into a trail. Turn left on Route 178 and follow it to Tyne Valley, where you will pick up Route 12 and follow it to the turning to Green Park Provincial Park.

CHARLOTTETOWN

DISTANCE: 37 km	**OTHER FACTORS:** Tricky left
TIME: 2 hrs	turn from the Trans-Canada to
DIFFICULTY: Easy to Moderate	Route 248 at North River.

PUTTING LEGS TO WORDS

Sometimes you have the feeling (well . . . I do, anyway) that a good bicycle ride is a means of putting legs to words. That is, you seek something you've read. For years, I've been looking for the experience of John Berger's field. Here is what Berger writes about a field in his book, *About Looking*:

> Shelf of a field, green, within easy reach, the grass on it not yet high, papered with blue sky through which yellow has grown to make pure green, the surface colour of what the basin of the world contains, attendant field, shelf between sky and sea, fronted with a curtain of printed trees, friable at its edges, the corners of it rounded, answering the sun with heat, shelf on a wall through which from time to time a cuckoo is audible, shelf on which she keeps the invisible and intangible jars of her pleasure, field that I have always known, I am lying raised up on one elbow wondering whether in any direction I can see beyond where you stop. The wire around you is the horizon.

His field is not anywhere in Prince Edward Island, of course, as you have undoubtedly noted. The cuckoo. In fact, John Berger is a British novelist and art critic who happens to live in France. His field is in France.

Never mind. I found my field not far from Charlottetown. You may find yours, too, not far off. But when I found my field it was still too early in the year to lie in the grass, and in fact I simply squatted down beside my bike and took a quadruped's low view across the damp brown field to the sea beyond. A dog's view, if you like. All fields in Prince Edward Island are tilted toward the sea. It is impossible not to sniff the air for the fugitive scents and cool aroma of the sea.

Back to being human (upright beside the bicycle), I fondled the word *pastoral* and thought that perhaps only the *pastoral* landscape invokes the word *graceful* — with its theological implications and its suggestions of pleasing movement: the clouds shift lazily over the field, the sky, the sea.

Then I cycled back to the old harbour town — which is also graceful, in its own way.

Where to Stay

There are two superior bed and breakfast establishments (of different personalities) right on this loop, as well as a private campground.

The campground was not yet open when I cycled past — I was very early in the season — but it certainly looked promising and worth examining further, and you might want to do that. It is called the Holiday Haven and is located on Route 248 (the old Ferry Road — there is no ferry), 2 km from Cornwall, 11 km from Charlottetown. It has hot showers and flush toilets and advertises shaded sites, clam-digging and a river beach. Bilingual service is available, and it is open from June 1 through October 1. *Holiday Haven Campground, Box 129, Cornwall, Prince Edward Island, C0A 1H0; (902) 566-2421; (winter) (902) 838-3385.*

Almost directly across from Holiday Haven on Route 248 is Chez Nous, a three-star bilingual bed and breakfast of modern furnishings (contemporary paintings on the walls) and serious musical atmosphere. Debussy on the music stand. A bountiful breakfast is advertised, with a different menu every morning. The third night is half-price. Open May 15 through October 31. *Chez Nous, Paul & Sandi Gallant, Ferry Road, R.R. #4, Cornwall, Prince Edward Island C0A 1H0; (902) 566-2779.*

The Elmwood Heritage Inn (three-and-a-half stars) is a Victorian mansion converted into an impressive bed and breakfast, located just off North River Road near Victoria Park in Charlottetown itself. It is a fifteen-minute walk to the Confederation Centre of the Arts and downtown. Victoria Park is at the foot of the street, right on the harbour. The Elmwood was built in 1889 for Arthur Peters (one of the grandsons of Samuel Cunard, who founded the famous steamship line), who was himself once premier of Prince Edward Island. The accommodations are gracious, spacious and elegant — the quilts are especially impressive — and the host is proud of his popovers. There is fresh baking everyday. Reservations are *required.* No smoking; open all year round. *Elmwood Heritage Inn, P.O. Box 3128, Charlottetown, Prince Edward Island C1A 7N8; (902) 368-3310.*

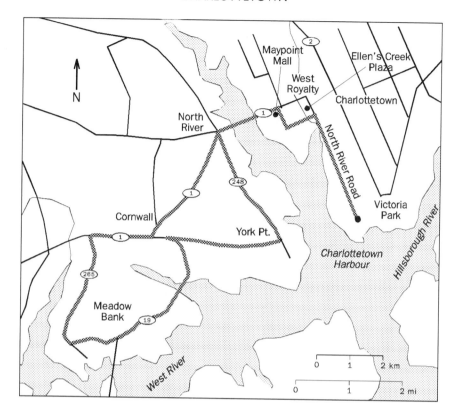

Bicycle Shop

There is an excellent bicycle shop in Charlottetown, MacQueen's, at 430 Queen Street, for repairs and rentals; (902) 368-2453.

The Ride

This ride is suitable for all kinds of bicycles.

I began the ride near the Elmwood Heritage Inn, which is near the foot of the North River Road, which is near Victoria Park, in Charlottetown. This is a ride which takes you from the town into the countryside with a minimum of fuss.

Ride northwesterly out the North River Road to the adjacent community of West Royalty, and turn left on the Beech Grove Road at the Ellen's Creek mini-plaza. There is a prominent Dunkin' Donut shop. Follow the curves of Beech Grove Road through suburbia to the first Stop sign. Turn right (northwesterly) at the Stop sign and cycle past apartment buildings on your right and a field on your left. The end of this short stretch of road will twist around the Maypoint Mall. Twist with it — and find yourself at some traffic lights at the Trans-Canada

Highway across from the Vehicle Disinfection Station. Turn left (southwesterly) at these lights. You may have to wait a moment for a car to come along and activate them. I did. Careful now: you are on the Trans-Canada, which has a good broad paved shoulder, but a good bit of traffic, too. Cycle along the Trans-Canada across the North River causeway to the community of North River, and turn left at the next set of lights onto the York Point Road. Be especially careful here. This is a busy intersection on a busy highway, and you will have to get out into the left-turn lane at the light in order to use the left-turn signal. You are on Route 248 travelling in a southerly direction toward York Point. There is a picnic table at the York Point Community Centre, which is beyond the farm where a windsock has been put out for the ducks. I liked that. You can stop at the community centre and think about ducks. The York Point Road will come to a T of sorts. That is to say, the paved road will turn right. You want the paved road. It is still Route 248, but now it is called the Ferry Road. (You are now approximately 10 km [6 mi] from your Charlottetown start.) Ride westerly along the Ferry Road (past Chez Nous and Holiday Haven) to Cornwall on the Trans-Canada Highway. You will see the Cornwall Post Office directly across the Trans-Canada Highway. Here you make a hairpin turn left onto Route 19 and follow Route 19 through the pastoral landscape until you come to Route 265, directing you to Clyde River. Turn right in a northerly direction toward the community of Clyde River on Route 265 until you meet the Trans-Canada again. Turn right (northeasterly) and ride on the broad paved shoulder of the Trans-Canada to the Maypoint Mall, where you return to Charlottetown the way you came out: on the twisty road to the Stop sign, Beech Grove Road to North River Road, and North River Road to Victoria Park or the Elmwood Heritage Inn.

STANHOPE and DALVAY

DISTANCE: 39 km (24 mi)	**OTHER FACTORS:** That
TIME: 2 hrs	awkward stretch of gravel, and
DIFFICULTY: Easy to Moderate	the wind off the sea.

Two Poor Little Rich Girls and One Glum Smuggler

Ms. Luxe will never forgive me. I was playing Joe Spartan on this trip and therefore Ms. Luxe missed the opportunity of sashaying down the grand staircase of the great inn of Dalvay By The Sea. Ms. Luxe is especially fond of sashaying, and good at it, too. Southern belles are born with a sashay in their hips. And a good sashay — while wonderful anywhere — is nowhere seen at as fine an advantage as it is descending a grand stairway, preferably to a crowd of elegantly dressed, admiring, mostly wealthy males taking note and making judgements, frequently with drink in hand. Imagine this in the nineteenth century; these chaps have steely eyes.

That's at the Dalvay By The Sea Inn. But Ms. Luxe missed her opportunity.

And I nearly did as well. I was exploring the north coast of Prince Edward Island, looking for a likely spot to cycle, and inevitably I came to the tourist area of Cavendish Beach. I hate Cavendish Beach. It is characterized by fast fried food joints and cute plastic critters by the hundreds leaping at you with terrible inviting grins right out of the moulds. It is enough to make you barf. So when I wheeled into the ticket kiosk at the entrance to Prince Edward Island National Park at Cavendish Beach, I was not in a good mood. "I'm here out of a sense of duty," I said to the girl in the kiosk. "I hate this place."

I admit, she was somewhat taken aback — but she recovered quickly, a credit to the Canadian National Park Service. She deserves a merit increment. She said: "It's better at the other end of the park — at Brackley Beach."

I thanked her as best I could, made a U-turn around the kiosk, and went to Brackley Beach. She was right. Nature makes a comeback at Brackley Beach. That is, you can see the sea and breathe the air and look at the world as it kind of began, before it was improved with plastic gewgaws and cute food.

At Brackley Beach there is some distance to the world. The nearby beach at the Stanhope Campground is clearly a favourite with parents, and no wonder. It is so vast that you can keep an eye on the little darlings while out of earshot of their exultations. They can scream their little heads off. They like it, too. Moreover, there is a fine National Park campground at Stanhope Beach — where I stayed — and a little farther on, near the eastern end of the park, at Dalvay beach, Dalvay By The Sea Inn, with its grandeur and its stories of self-made millionaires and poor little rich girls and a glum smuggler of another time, and a grand staircase.

The inn was once the private summer estate of one Alexander McDonald, born in Scotland near Inverness in the early years of the nineteenth century, who came to Cincinnati, Ohio, in the middle of the century and made a fortune in starch and oil. He and his brother started out in oil by selling kerosene, then branched out into what became Standard Oil of Ohio and then Standard Oil of Kentucky, and the money rolled in in great amounts. Some of it washed up on Prince Edward Island where McDonald found a seascape which reminded him of his innocent days as a boy in Scotland. Summer homes among the rich are frequently memories of innocence.

McDonald had married (in 1862) a certain Laura Palmer, and they had a daughter, also named Laura, who married one Edmund Stello, who was the son of the American Ambassador to Rome. This is how he is best described; it may be the only description possible of him. Remember him; we are slipping into the novels of Henry James and Edith Wharton. Alexander McDonald's daughter and her husband (the son of the Ambassador to Rome) had two children, both girls: Laura (Laura III) and Helena. When the girls' mother (Laura II) died in 1895, the girls went to live with their grandparents, and they continued to live with Grandfather McDonald after the death of Grandmother Laura McDonald in 1903. When Grandfather McDonald, the Scottish boy who became an American millionaire, died in turn in 1910, the girls inherited, together, 17 million dollars (U.S). They were very rich.

And they found themselves with a problem not uncommon in their circles at that time: you can see evidence of it in Newport, Rhode Island, should you visit there, or in the novels of Henry James and Edith Wharton. (A bibliography is available in *To Marry An English Lord*, by Gail MacColl and Carol McD. Wallace.) And you can see the problem right here in the Dalvay By The Sea Inn, as you descend the grand staircase. The problem is this: how should one live if one is rich as a lord, a duke, a king? What sort of dwelling is suitable? What sort of mate ought one to have?

Although the girls had suitors back in Cincinnati, Ohio, the suitors lacked *cachet*. One of them was from *Dayton, Ohio*, for heaven's sakes! No, if you were as rich as European nobility, clearly you needed some sort of certification of your worth, your superiority. This might best be accomplished by marrying some chap with wonderful blood-lines — which was frequently just fine with European nobility, who had great blood but no income to speak of. Young Laura and young Helena set off for Europe to better themselves. They were received with open arms in Europe. Helena, for example, was the darling of the press in London, which reported that she had bought two hundred pairs of shoes in New York and that she bathed in a tub of solid gold! What *is* it about shoes that so attracts money? And clearly she was attractive if she bathed in a tub of solid gold. Would a plain girl have dared?

And they met their men. Helena got hers first. He was Prince Michel Charles Murat, the great-grandson of Napoleon's most famous marshal. Laura, the elder, moved on to Italy, where she bagged Prince Francisco Rospigliosi, whose family seems to have dated back to the Middle Ages. As whose doesn't? Rospigliosi and wife honeymooned in the Arctic because it was the only part of the world the chap hadn't yet seen.

If you have read your Henry James and Edith Wharton, you know that things were bound to go wrong, and they did, and of course money was the crux of the matter.

Prince Murat turned out to be a gambler. Worse, he was not a good one. He also turned out to be a forger. Worse still, he was no better at that. He was caught and sent to jail. When he was released he pawned some jewellery. Worst of all, it turned out that the jewellery belonged to a woman not his wife. The chap was an utter rotter. Helena died of shame in Paris at the age of thirty-eight.

Laura's prince seemed to be the better of the two, but of course it costs a good deal to support a family, and he and Laura had to turn to Laura's father — remember him? the son of the American Ambassador to Rome? — for some money from their inheritance, which he was administering. It wasn't there. It had disappeared. Being the son of the American Ambassador to Rome had not (apparently) equipped him to deal with investments in railroads, and the money just took a train and never came back. Laura was forced to charge her own father with *embezzlement*, but the suit got her nothing. She returned to the U.S. and opened a cosmetics shop in New York, but it was the Depression; the plain look became fashionable and the shop failed.

Laura returned to Europe and her prince, but in 1938 Prince Rospigliosi asked for a divorce in order to marry somebody else, and while he was at it, he wanted the nearly four million dollars (U.S.) which he had been promised for marrying Laura in the first place. Too bad, it was all gone. She had turned out to be a bad investment. Laura and her two daughters returned to the U.S. and disappeared into the vast continent.

But what of Dalvay By The Sea?

It had somehow escaped the hands of the McDonald heirs at the start of the Depression and came into the possession of Captain Ned Dick, who was the fellow who first operated the mansion as a hotel. He made his fortune smuggling booze. He was uncommonly good at that, and his ship, the *Nellie J. Banks*, was famous along the coast and in the fogs between St. Pierre-et-Miquelon (where the booze was purchased legally because these islands were and are the possessions of France) and Prince Edward Island. Songs are sung about the *Nellie J. Banks* to this day.

But Ned Dick had a failing. Oh, not the booze. He drank his product to glorious excess, but that wasn't the failing. His failing was that he gave credit. And his customers didn't pay. You can see his glum untutored letter of lament to his supplier in St. Pierre posted at the Dalvay By The Sea Inn. It is framed and affixed to the wall, where it serves as yet another cautionary tale.

There are serious lessons to be learned here.

The word *sashay* is a variant on the French word *chasser*, to glide — as in a dance. Now you know. Amanda Wingfield, the mother in Tennessee Williams's *The Glass Menagerie*, uses the word to explain to her shy daughter — another Laura! — how she attracted "gentlemen callers": "See how I sashayed around the ballroom, Laura? . . . for my gentlemen callers."

Where to Stay

The Stanhope Campground, 8 km (5 mi) east of Brackley Beach, is everything a campground should be — and therefore you will want to be there early. *Reservations are NOT accepted.* It is open from 14 June through 27 September. It has wooded sites, hot showers, flush toilets, kitchen shelters and washing machines — but no dryers. *Prince Edward Island National Park, District Superintendent, Environment Canada, Canadian Parks Service, Box 487, Charlottetown, Prince Edward Island C1A 7L1; (902) 672-2211.*

Dalvay By The Sea Inn and Restaurant — to give the establish-

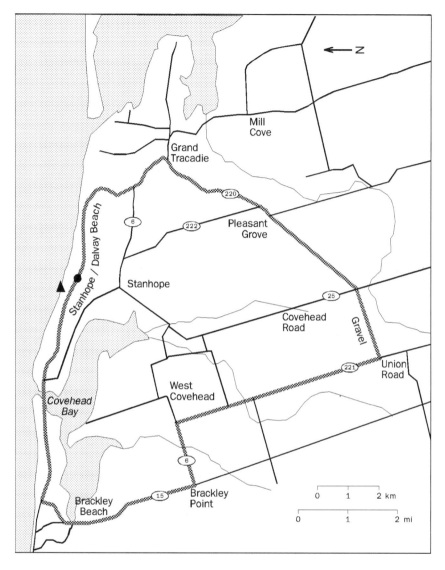

ment its full name — is something extraordinary, and of course it is expensive. Hobnobbing with ghostly millionaires will cost you something. This is a hotel for a most special occasion. (Ask *not* to be put in the former servants' quarters.) You will find it listed in the Prince Edward Island Visitors' Guide under Grand Tracadie in Queens County, but in fact it is just down the way from Brackley Beach and right near the eastern exit of the Prince Edward Island National Park. It is open from mid-June to mid-September. The living is elegant and the food said to be extraordinary. More to the point, if you have somehow neglected to bring along a bicycle, you can rent one here — and the manager, David Thompson (no relation), is a keen mountain-biker. *Dalvay By The Sea Inn, David R. Thompson, Box 8, Little York, Prince Edward Island C0A 1P0; (902) 672-2048; (winter) (902) 672-2546.*

The Ride

A mountain bike is recommended for this ride because of one short stretch of thick gravel — where you may find yourself reminded of the old horse term, *headstrong* — but if you are willing to walk those 2 km (1 mi), you can use a ten-speed road bike.

Turn right (easterly) out of either the Stanhope Campground or the grounds of Dalvay By The Sea Inn, and follow the Gulf Shore Parkway to the eastern exit of the Prince Edward Island National Park. (You may exit and return to the park on a bicycle without stopping at the kiosk.) When you exit the park you will find yourself on Route 6. You will follow it perhaps 1 km (.5 mi) to Route 220, which goes off to your right (southwesterly) *before* you reach the community of Grand Tracadie. There was no sign on Route 6 warning of the appearance of Route 220, but when I looked down the likely road I could see Route 220 clearly marked. Turn right on Route 220 and study the sign and continue straight. The surface is chipseal. Ignore the opportunity to turn on Route 222 at Pleasant Grove, and continue straight on to the junction with Route 25 — for which there is also no sign. A sign across the road will point you, however, to the Union Road. You want to take the Union Road. Within a couple of hundred yards the pavement gives way to gravel. Probably has something to do with politics. This is the awkward stretch. You can manage. Stay with the tough stuff until you come to the T, which is Route 221, a much-patched asphalt road on which you turn right, and go north to the next T, which is Route 6. Turn left (west) on Route 6 for 2 km (1 mi) to the next T, which is Route 15. Turn right (north) on Route 15 toward Brackley Beach. Ice cream available here. You might want to stop to talk to the friendly folk at the Brackley Beach tourist information centre. In the park turn right (east) on the Parkway and ride on the wide paved shoulder along the beaches, gulping in sea air, to the campground or the hotel.

Growf

The campsite I had chosen was level, shaded, breezy, clean, close to the washrooms (but not too close), and not on anyone's obvious path to anywhere else. No power-lines overhead.

Perfect, you might say. So I said; so I thought.

Not quite. There was a bird in the tree over my head. The bird was unhappy with me. Perhaps he did not like cyclists on principle. He was a very big bird. He was a very black bird. He was a very big black bird. He was a raven. A raven is bigger than a crow which is bigger than a grackle which is bigger than a starling. Not a laugh in the lot. A raven on a tree-limb looks like the *maître d'* at a restaurant where they refuse to serve you and don't have any food anyway. A raven can fix you with a mean eye. What's more, ravens can learn to talk.

Yes they can! And this particular large ugly bird was obviously irritated with my presence and was emitting annoying sounds of endless complaint, on and on and on. It took me a while to understand his syntax, and the discovery was disconcerting. He had been taught to talk by a dog.

What's more, it was obvious that the dog who taught the bird was a querulous mean-mouthed yappy discontented irksome canine who hated everyone and was going to let everyone know about it. No, he *would not* be quiet. The dog was too cowardly to bark and too mean to shut up. He sat incarnate in the bird overhead and growled, whined, lamented. Grooowwwwffff. He had no intention of letting up, ever. What he wanted was justice. No, more than justice! Growwwwffffffip. What he wanted was something better for himself. No, not just something better! What he wanted was comfort. That was it. He wanted comfort. And moreover he wanted nothing to have ever gone wrong ever. Growwwfffffffffffowieeeeffff. No, not just the future had to be improved; the past had to be improved. If the past wasn't improved he was going to sit here all night and tell me about it. Why did I think the Park Service put in lights? For him, that's why, so he could tell me about his hard life. Growwwwffffffyip. Well, couldn't I figure that out for *myself*? He thought I had more brains than that. And no, I could not even talk back to him because that was Bird Abuse — and he took up that theme. Bird Abuse, Bird Abuse, Bird Abuse. Listen to me. I can keep this up all night long. Bird Abuse,

Bird Abuse, Bird Abuse, Bird Abuse, Bird Abuse, Bird Abuse, Bird Abuse, Bird Abuse, Bird Abuse, **Here comes the Ranger** Bird Abuse Bird Abuse Bird Abuse Bird Abuse Bird Abuse Bird Abuse Growwwwwfffffffipp Bird Abuse Bird Abuse Bird Abuse **Evening** Bird Abuse Bird Abuse **Nice evening, eh?** Bird Abuse Bird Abuse Bird Abuse Growwffffip Bird Abuse Bird Abuse **That's a raven** Bird Abuse Bird Abuse Bird Abuse Growff Bird Abuse **Yep, he's a loud one** Bird Abuse Bird Abuse Bird Abuse **He does sound like a dog, doesn't he** Bird Abuse Bird Abuse Bird Abuse Bird Abuse Bird Abuse **Well, have a good evening** Bird Abuse Bird Abuse Bird Abuse Growwwfffffipipi-pipipip Bird Abuse Bird Abuse Bird Abuse Bird Abuse Bird Abuse **You weren't thinking of throwing a rock at that bird, were you?** Bird Abuse Bird Abuse Bird Abuse Bird Abuse **See you later, I'll be making rounds quite frequently unannounced** Bird Abuse Bird Abuse Bird Abuse Bird Abuse Bird Abuse Bird Abuse Nyah Nyah Nyah Nyah Nyah Bird Abuse Bird Abuse Bird Abuse Growwwwfffffip Bird Abuse Bird Abuse Woof Woof Woof Nyah Nyah Nyah Nyah.

PANMURE ISLAND

DISTANCE: 47 km (30 mi)	**DIFFICULTY:** Easy
TIME: 2 hrs 30 min	**OTHER FACTORS:** None

Where The Buffalo Roam

Perhaps you have done this sort of thing yourself. I shan't be surprised if you have. Cyclists have a propensity this way. You look up at the sky out of which rain is pouring down, and you think: it looks like it's clearing up; I can get in a couple of hours before supper.

O foolish person.

Join me. I went cycling in the rain from Panmure Island to Murray River, passed the buffalo on my way back, considered the railway station with longing and envy, and returned to the campground soaked through. My boots squished for days afterwards. I had a wonderful time.

Well, what's a little rain? What's a great deal of rain? Remember when you were little and you got soaked in a summer storm and how good it felt? It feels good. You are worshipping water, and later you will worship fire, and soon you will be considering your spiritual state. Bicycling is a metaphysical activity. Sometimes.

Besides, there is no shelter whatever between Panmure Island and Murray River, and not much between Murray River and Buffaloland (honest — I am not making this up) Provincial Park, and precious little there, so if it should happen to be raining the day you decide to ride this route, the only choice you have is staying put in the campground — which, to a cyclist, is no choice at all.

I rode in the rain to Murray River. It is a cozy little community with a harbour full of masts and a pleasant little gift shop created out of what was once a general store, and a little seafood restaurant where you eat off paper plates and the portions are generous. I ate well and left Murray River in the rain and cycled off to see the buffalo.

I did not see the buffalo. It was raining. They were elsewhere. But I peered into the distance and believed they were there.

How did the buffalo come to be here?

Do not believe stories you might hear of buffalo swimming the Northumberland Strait. Such stories are not to be believed, especially if embellished with lovely maidens clinging to the beasts' shaggy fur.

The buffalo — and yes, I know the proper name is bison, but you don't say that, do you, and neither do I — were a gift from the government of Alberta to the government of Prince Edward Island. It is the kind of gift delivered with much bonhomie and handshakes and laughter. Just who is laughing at what is a matter of some debate.

But imagine it: the Alberta officials have flown off back to the land of the Big Sky and oil wells, and the fellows from Prince Edward Island are contemplating their inheritance.

One says: "I suppose steaks are out of the question."

Another says: "They'll never pull a buggy."

A third says: "What will be the effect on the fishing industry?"

A fourth says: "We'll have to build a park."

And so they have. Buffaloland Provincial Park has no facilities except a picnic table. All right: two picnic tables. They weren't going to go overboard on this project. There is a fenced pathway down to a viewing platform where you can look out upon the distance and spy the beasts at their pleasure. I saw no beasts. Perhaps a deer under the trees way off there, and I'm not sure about that. You can stand under the viewing platform if it is raining, but you will find it leaks.

On the way back to Panmure Island Provincial Campground — O, the rain on my face, the vigour of it! — I spied, off to the left, an old railway coach and, beyond it, a railway station — but no tracks. Had they perhaps been pulled up hereabouts? Was there perhaps an abandoned railbed turned into a trail on which I might add mud to my water? No. I enquired of a passing motorist. A fellow bought the railway coach and had it dragged here; the same fellow purchased the old railway station — a classic station, with a steep overhanging roof (so that passengers could shelter from the rain) and windows all around.

I envied that fellow. Were I that fellow I would be writing these words in that place even now. I am not that fellow and I am writing elsewhere.

I rode back to Panmure Island Provincial Campground and peeled off my soggy clothes. Mosquitoes immediately colonized my boots. It was a rainy summer. It was a lovely ride.

Buffalo! Who would have thought it?

Where to Stay

Panmure Island Provincial Campground has everything a cyclist might need (hot showers, flush toilets) or want (laundry facilities), as well as a supervised ocean beach. It is located on Route 347, north of Gaspereaux. It is open between June 26 and September 7. Reserva-

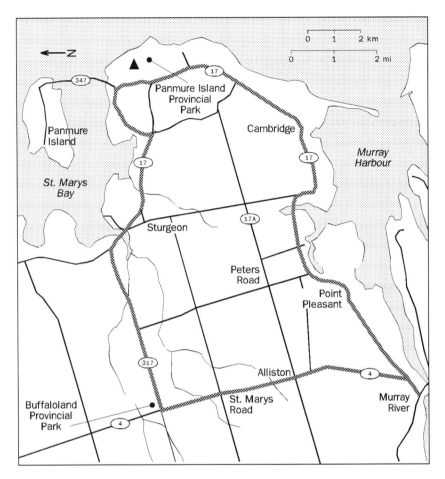

tions accepted after April 1. *Panmure Island Provincial Campground, Department of Tourism and Parks Division East, Box 2000, Charlotte-town, Prince Edward Island C1A 7N8; (902) 838-4719; (winter) (902) 652-2356.*

Lady Catherine's Bed and Breakfast is a most welcoming establishment on Route 17 between Gaspereaux and Murray Harbour. This is a three-star accommodation which is accustomed to cyclists — and in fact has bicycles available if somehow you have neglected to bring your own. It is open all year. *Lady Catherine's Bed and Breakfast, R.R. #4, Montague, Prince Edward Island C0A 1R0; (902) 962-3426.*

The Ride.

All of this route is paved, so it is duck soup (please excuse that — but you will understand) for a ten-speed bike or hybrid or mountain bike.

I rode from the Panmure Island Provincial Campground to Route 17, and turned left (south) on Route 17 and followed it past Lady Catherine's Bed and Breakfast all the way to the outskirts of Murray River. I ignored 17A. The junction of Route 17 and Route 4 is perhaps 1 km (.5 mi) above the village of Murray River, but you will probably want to visit Murray River for food and drink or to see the sights. Return to the junction of Route 4 and 17 and follow Route 4 north to Buffaloland Provincial Park, which is at the junction of Route 4 and Route 317. Turn right (east) on Route 317 and continue past the private railway car and its station to Route 17. Turn right (southeasterly) on Route 17 and to the signs to Panmure Island Provincial Park on Route 347. Turn left (north) on Route 347 to the campground.

ELMIRA

Ride One	Ride Two
DISTANCE: 25 km (15.5 mi)	**DISTANCE:** 50 km (31 mi)
TIME: 1 hr 15 min	**TIME:** 2 hrs 30 min
DIFFICULTY: Easy	**DIFFICULTY:** Moderate

Tea?

When you stop to think about it, there was probably no great practical need for a railway in Prince Edward Island in the first place. What place is better suited to coastal transportation by steamer, or horse-and-buggy on inland roads, or bicycle?

But of course practical considerations are rarely all that important in human affairs, and in the middle of the nineteenth century it was a matter of Pride that every little political or geographical unit in the world should have its own railway. Why, without a Railway we'd be at the end of Nowhere and no way to get here! It was much like the impulse which demanded that every little country in the world have its own airline in the 1950s.

The results could have been predicted, and probably were. No one cared. Prince Edward Island went broke building its railway — and in fact Prince Edward Island entered into Confederation with Canada in 1873 because it was, for all intents and purposes, bankrupt. It was bankrupt because of the railway. Thus is history shaped.

Never mind. It was a lovely little railway, with many salutary effects, as you will see. Passenger service was gone completely by 1971, and the last freight rolled along the rails in 1989, but you can see easily enough where the old rail line meandered from one end to the other, and yes, the old line would make a wonderful bicycle path. What a holiday! Probably the best cycling in North America — but of course it is the usual story: the adjacent landowners want the railway land for themselves, and therefore Prince Edward Island is deeply into the common dispute between dogs-in-the-manger (the landowners) and those people who want a linear park for everyone — including tourists, of course. Guess which side I'm on.

Never mind. Ignore what might be and look at what is. At Elmira you will find a museum to the small glories of the island railway, housed (naturally) in the station which was once the eastern terminus of the line. There are photographs galore and old notices — one of which advertises one of the social delights of the railway years. It was the Tea.

A word of explanation is probably necessary. As the word is used in this context it is closer to the British use of "High Tea," which means a major meal at the end of the day with something "savoury" (by which is meant, often, fried sausages) and probably potatoes. This in turn is not to be confused with "Tea" served in Canadian hotels invoking the British colonial past (the Empress in Victoria, British Columbia, comes to mind) which will feature cups of tea, of course, but also many sweets: biscuits (cookies), crumpets (pancakes of a sort full of bubble-holes swamped with butter), and scones. This sort of Tea emphasizes the British genteel traditions which are so popular on the U.S. Public Broadcasting System. The Afternoon Tea is usually served at 4 p.m.; the High Tea at 6 p.m.

But the Mammoth Tea (advertised all across the island for July 11, 1912) at Elmira was something different yet again. It was an all-afternoon eating festival. People came from everywhere to eat and talk with their neighbours from everywhere else. You might imagine that people knew one another better in those days than we do now, and that the entire island was one large neighbourhood. It must have been great fun; it's a pity it's gone.

You will find that you can ride some of the old railbed out of Elmira, but not as much as you might, or as you might have expected. You will find ads boasting that 25 km (15.5 mi) of rail-trail are available, but in fact you find no more than 2 km (1 mi) usable.

That's a shame, but not a disaster. The country roads hereabouts are excellent for cycling, and if you want that different sense of Time, that pastoral rhythm tuned to cows and crops, together with a cool breeze off the vast sea, then this is the ride for you.

Where to Stay
There are two excellent provincial campgrounds —one on this loop, the other near it — both on the water, one on the north shore of the island and one on the south.

Red Point Provincial Park is an excellent campground on the south coast, on Route 16, 13 km (8 mi) east of Souris. (Souris is the port of departure for the ferry to the Magdalen Islands/Îles de la Madeleine.) It has hot showers, flush toilets, fireplaces and a supervised beach. It is open from June 19 through September 7. Reservations are accepted after April 1. *Red Point Provincial Park, Department of*

Tourism and Parks, Parks Division East, Box 2000, Charlottetown, Prince Edward Island C1A 7N8; (902) 357-2463; (winter) (902) 652-2356.

Campbells Cove Provincial Park is another excellent campground, but on the north coast, right on the loop of Route 16, 5 km (3 mi) west of Elmira. It has hot showers, flush toilets, fireplaces, and a beach. It is open from June 26 through September 7. Reservations are accepted after April 1. *Campbells Cove Provincial Park, Department of Tourism and Parks, Parks Division East, Box 2000, Charlottetown, Prince Edward Island C1A 7N8; (902) 357-2067; (winter) (902) 652-2356.*

In Souris is the four-star Matthew House Inn, a restored Victorian home which enjoys a superior reputation as an inn — and which was full the night that Ms. Luxe and I needed it. Hard luck for us, likely. It advertises all sorts of attractions for cyclists, including box lunches, candlelight dining, laundry facilities — and bicycle rentals. It is open from June 15 through October 1. *Matthew House Inn, Box 151, Souris, Prince Edward Island C0A 2B0; (902) 687-3461.*

Ride One

You will probably want to use a mountain bicycle for this route, but a hybrid would do quite well, and even a ten-speed might be used. The dirt road is packed hard enough so that even heavy rains (the day I rode it) didn't make it muddy. This ride is described from Campbells Cove Provincial Park, but of course you can start from any place on the loop. The loop is comparatively short, but can be lengthened (as I indicate) quite easily.

I left Campbells Cove Provincial Park and turned left (northeasterly) on Route 16 and ignored the turning to North Lake and stayed to the right until I came to the sign directing me to Elmira. Turn right (southeasterly) to the Elmira Railway Station Museum — where there are washrooms. If you ask about the rail-trail at the museum you will be advised to walk your bike alongside the remaining tracks for a couple of hundred yards until you come to the prepared trail. Good advice. Which I ignored and had a merry time bouncing along the dog-track alongside the old railway tracks. Well, it was a test; I passed. Then the improved rail-trail begins, and very nice it is, too, for 2 km (1 mi). Then you come to an intersecting road, the Munns Road, and on the other side of the Munns Road the rail-trail continues, but it is considered suitable only for hiking. Never mind. Turn left on the Munns Road and ride south until you come in no time at all to an intersecting dirt road. Turn right, southwesterly, on this dirt road. This is dirt — not gravel — but hard-packed, and on a mountain bike you can fair fly. Stay on the dirt road through wooded country until you come to the first paved intersecting road, which is Route 302. Turn right, northerly, on Route 302 and ride to the T at Priest Pond, where you meet Route 16. Turn right, northeasterly, on Route 16 and return to the campground.

Ride Two

This is an extension of Ride One. I drove this but did not cycle it. All right, I'll admit it: it was pouring down rain. I was soaked through. You can add as much as 25 km (15.5 mi) *more* by following Route 16 northeasterly after you leave the campground, including the road to North Lake Harbour, which is a spot renowned for deep-sea fishing and huge tuna. A world-record tuna was caught here in 1979. It weighed 680 kg (1496 lbs). You will find yourself back on Route 16. Follow it around the eastern tip of Prince Edward Island at East Point and then you will find yourself heading southwest, still on Route 16. You will come to a road called Route 16A, off to your right, which will direct you northeasterly to Elmira, where you can stop at the Railway Museum, or pick up the dirt road here instead of off the Munns Road. Take the dirt road to Route 302 and thence to Route 16 on the north side of the island, and thence back to Campbell Cove Provincial Park.

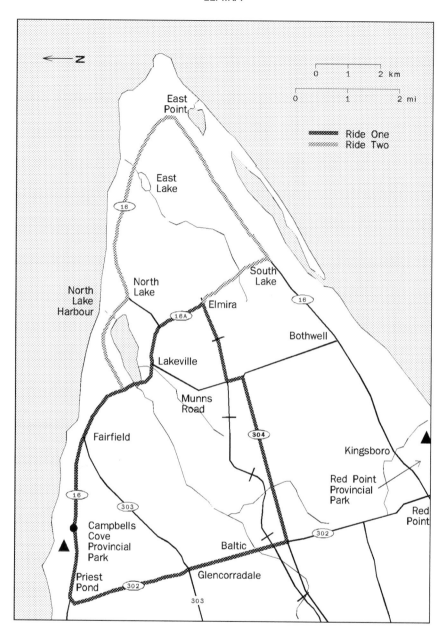

N

| 0 | 1 | 2 km |
| 0 | 1 | 2 mi |

Ride One
Ride Two

East Point

East Lake

16

North Lake Harbour

North Lake

South Lake

Elmira

16

16A

Bothwell

Lakeville

Munns Road

304

Fairfield

Kingsboro

Red Point Provincial Park

16

303

Campbells Cove Provincial Park

Baltic

Red Point

302

Priest Pond

302

Glencorradale

303

MAGDALEN ISLANDS /
ÎLES DE LA MADELEINE

1. Cap aux Meules
2. Havre Aubert
3. Havre Aubert
4. Havre aux Maisons

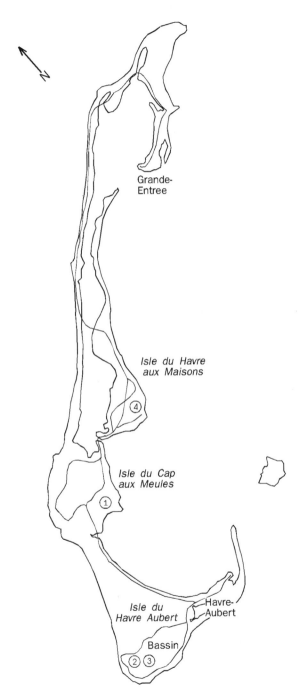

Grande-Entree

Isle du Havre
aux Maisons

Isle du Cap
aux Meules

Isle du
Havre Aubert

Havre-Aubert

Bassin

MAGDALEN ISLANDS / ÎLES DE LA MADELEINE

Ride One
DISTANCE: 30 km (18.5 mi)
TIME: 1 hr 30 min
DIFFICULTY: Easy

Ride Two
DISTANCE: 20 km (12 mi)
TIME: 1 hr
DIFFICULTY: Easy to Moderate
OTHER FACTORS: A real grunting climb out of the campground.

Ride Three
DISTANCE: 17 km (10.5 mi)
TIME: 1 hr
DIFFICULTY: Moderate to Difficult
OTHER FACTORS: Wind

Ride Four
DISTANCE: 17 km (10.5 mi); 37 km (23 mi) to Camping Gros-Cap
TIME: 1 hr; 2 hrs to Camping Gros-Cap
DIFFICULTY: Moderate
OTHER FACTORS: Gravel road uphill and downhill.

A World Away

We missed the ferry by eighteen feet. That was the measured length of our old van. You pay for vans by the foot (not the metre) and although we got to the ferry line-up at Souris, Prince Edward Island, by 1:30 in the afternoon — sailing was scheduled for 2 p.m. — there was not enough room for us. We should have reserved, and would have, had we known the number. Here it is: *(418) 986-3278. But* you must reserve 48 hours before the crossing you desire. We didn't know that. Now you do. Reservations are a very good idea, especially in the height of the summer season. Other numbers to call for information are (902) 687-2181 in Souris, or (418) 986-6600 in Cap-aux-Meules, the other terminus.

But we were left on the pier as the lovely white ship, the *Lucy Maud Montgomery*, set off for Îles de la Madeleine, or the Magdalen Islands. Usually the former, as you will see, because the isles are part of Québec, and Québec is stern about language.

Stymied, we stopped at the Red Point Provincial Park campground some 10 km (6 mi) from the ferry dock at Souris. It is a nice campground: flush toilets, hot showers. That night there was one hell of a storm, and we peered out the window of our van as the sea was stirred up, flipped over, and flung against the shore, and the wind howled. A tent in the near distance was one moment a taut and cunning little structure, straining against the wind, and the next moment a sodden heap of sheets on the ground.

The trip from Souris to Cap-aux-Meules (Grindstone Island) on the big white beautiful *Lucy Maud Montgomery* is by definition a ferry ride (the hull is stuffed with cars, vans, semi-trailer trucks), but the trip takes five to six hours (usually) and is less like a ferry ride than it is like a Voyage, or a Crossing. Moreover, you are leaving an English-speaking shore in Prince Edward Island, for a French-speaking destination. Mostly French-speaking. (There are two small English-speaking communities in Îles de la Madeleine/Magdalen Islands.) For our Crossing the sea was kind, and the ship (apart from the hull) was uncrowded; the food was good.

We met the children waiting for the ferry. We were in line four hours before sailing, this time. We read and mended stuff, improved this or that. I studied the manual for my new bicycle. The "children," as we came to call them, or the "puppies," were a dozen young people, most of them in their early teens, on a bicycling holiday. They rode all sorts of bikes — touring bikes and mountain bikes — laden down with sleeping bags and tents. They left their support vehicles (two mini-vans and a trailer) behind on the pier at Souris — probably because of the expense, which can add up quickly, as you shall see — and came aboard as foot passengers with bicycles. If you are tenting, this is almost certainly the wise decision, but we were camping in the old van, and so we were stuck with it. You have to pay for the bicycle ($6.50), by the way, unless you have it inside your van, as I did. If you have a van. Calculate the van at 18 feet by $4.20, plus two adults at $28.75 each to get what we paid — $133.10. That's one-way, by the way, and the figures are for 1992. You might be wise to figure on an additional 5% to 10%.

We called the children "puppies" because of all that energy and joy and playfulness. With nothing else to do waiting for the ferry, they rode their bicycles around in circles. But when we saw them next, on the ferry, they were in a circle on the deck consuming teen food quickly in many crunches. Who was it who defined the three basic food groups for teenagers as *hamburgers, pizza, and potato chips*? But when we saw them again minutes later they were dossed down in their sleeping bags like hot dogs, catching up. Like puppies, they could fall asleep instantly, wherever they were. If they had tried to camp in the storm the night before, they needed their sleep. They awoke from their naps full of laughter, chatter and cheer. Later, we would look for them on the road — and found them, it seemed, always eating and laughing.

Travel on the *Lucy Maud Montgomery* is sea travel the way it used to be, long ago, in the days of the ocean liners. Which is to say that there is a restaurant (as well as a cafeteria) on board, with excellent food (you would expect the fish to be good, and it is) and excellent service, and a nice crisp wine available and not very expensive, either. There is also a bar, sometimes with live entertainment — and a smoking room, a TV lounge, a gift shop (of course) and a kiddie corner with a keeper. This is the civilized (remember that word?) way to travel.

So you dock at Cap-aux-Meules, which gives this particular island of the archipelago its name: Île du Cap aux Meules. In the English-language weather reports back on the mainland it is called Grindstone Island, which means the same thing. There was a time when grindstones were taken out of these cliffs. And just there you'll see the Irving Oil tanks. You'll see them again later at Grande-Entrée, and the more you cycle this region of the world — the Maritime provinces and Îles de la Madeleine — the more you will realize that the Irving interests have an unerring instinct for finding a lovely spot and there depositing their oil tanks. Well, they probably think their oil tanks are lovely — and I shall not gainsay them. I use Irving Oil. I carry an Irving credit card.

The Îles de la Madeleine/Magdalen Islands are an archipelago, of which six are connected by sand dunes. A road (Québec Route 199) uses these sand dunes to let you drive or ride the 65 km (40 mi) from the southwesterly tip at Havre-Aubert to the northeasterly tip at Grande-Entrée. A seventh island is Île d'Entrée (not to be confused with Grande-Entrée), which is the one you'll see first from the *Lucy Maud Montgomery* as you approach the isles. It is anomalous among the islands because it can be reached only by ferry (from Cap-aux-Meules) and because the language spoken there is English.

The word which occurs to me most often in the Magdalen Islands is the word *primary*. Primary colours — green hills, red sandstone cliffs, golden beaches, grey sea/blue sea/green sea everywhere as background. And it is not so much that life here is radically different from life on the mainland (not so very different, for example, from Québec life up the Saguenay), but there is less of what seems so easily to characterize our civilization right now.

It's easy to fool yourself, however. You will have the feeling, leaving the mainland, that you are going to a speck in the ocean, a stretch of sand dune in the sea (that part is true), with only the occasional weathered cottage. But what you will find — perhaps to your surprise — is a population of 14,000 people across these islands (more in the summer, I suspect), two new-car dealerships, *appts 4^1/2 à louer*, and many gas stations. There is a fine bicycle shop, Le Pédalier, at 365 Chemin Principal, Cap-aux-Meules ([418] 986-2965), where bicycle repairs are available, as well as rentals and purchases, in both official languages. There are several motels — but they are not chain motels. There are many *casse-croutes* (everyday, quick-food restaurants), but they will not be the familiar franchise operations of the mainland. There are different kinds of private campgrounds. The islands are Primary, not Primitive.

It occurs to me here (not for the first time, nor, I suspect, the last) that when you and I ride out on our bicycles we are engaging the world as directly as possible.

Why else would we do it?

If we simply wanted exercise we could have ridden exercise bicycles in front of our TVs. Yuck, you say, and rightly. Or we could *ride the numbers*, which is what many cyclists do. You can hear them come in from a ride saying, "Great day — got a hundred klicks," and therein notice their joy: it's in numbers. Not for us, likely.

These are not in fact very long rides. If you want numbers you'll have to cycle from Havre-Aubert to Grande-Entrée (65 km, 40 mi, one way) and back on Québec Route 199. It won't even get you your *century* in miles. You will get your exercise, however: the wind can be stiff, and it blows constantly — note the windmills at Dune-du-Sud.

Nope. I suspect you and I are here to hang around in the Sublime — to experience the vastness of the sea; the horizon which is as far as you can see, and, beyond that, only imagine. But that's what we mean by the *Sublime*, isn't it? We are overwhelmed by the size of nature, by its force; we are reminded of just how pitifully puny we are. The sea can remind you of that in a moment.

And art, much as I love art, can serve only as a reminder, no matter how huge the canvas, or loud the symphony, or long the book, because, let's face it, all art is reductionist. You look at a picture — a landscape or a seascape — and it is small. OK, so it's Barnett Newman's painting called "Voice of Fire" in the Canadian National Gallery in Ottawa — the one that caused so much consternation among the political oafs in the nation's capital, who were quick to volunteer that they could have done as well with a couple of gallons of paint and a roller. Uh-huh, but they *didn't*, did they. They didn't think of it. And they missed the point, anyway. What Barnett Newman is trying to remind us of (the best he can do is remind us, give us an experience of knowing, inside a building) is that Fire is stunning in its implications. Sublime.

So here we are, you and I, cycling out to put our turning wheels to the turning of the earth in the cosmos and find ourselves overwhelmed by the size and colour of what we find ourselves *in*. When we climb Chemin des Montants in Île du Havre aux Maisons, for example, and see beyond the green valley to the cliffs and the sea bashing the shore in explosions of white foam. We are going there to get the experience. Nothing else like it. And, just as in Isle Madame in Cape Breton (where I also babble on about this) we have to earn it with our legs.

You will learn a great deal about modern art here. I did, anyway. That is, looking out at the sea I thought of the paintings of Christopher Pratt of Newfoundland — how he looks out from his screened-in porch at the sea, and then looks directly at the sea, and soon is looking at the colours and horizontals of the sea — as he moves from pictorial art to abstract art, demonstrating the connections and the differences. It occurred to me that any picture of the sea without boats is abstract art, that the sea demonstrates abstraction.

And look what the people of these islands have done with their houses in their landscape/seascape world: wonderful flashes of colour — like irises in a green field. There *are* irises in green fields. But the people who live here have softened the colours a bit (as if the primary colours of red sandstone and blue sea, sky, green hills, were the properties of nature, and humans ought to have something more subtle and witty) into pastels of raspberry, mauve, violet, chartreuse. Like the wild strawberries you can find in the grass around the parking lot at the Musée de la Mer at Havre-Aubert.

Finally, shipwrecks. There have been many shipwrecks on these islands in the last couple of centuries; nobody knows quite how many. Over four hundred. On August 24, 1873, for example, the entire American and Canadian fishing fleets were sunk in Baie de Plaisance near Havre-Aubert, forty-seven vessels in one night. (There is a map near the Purser's wicket on the *Lucy Maud Montgomery* which indicates the approximate location of many of the wrecks. You can buy a different map of area wrecks at the Musée de la Mer in

Havre-Aubert; I did.) And cycling toward L'Étang-du-Nord on Île Cap aux Meules, I noticed in the distance what I assumed to be an Irving oil refinery until I came close — and cycled out to look at it, because the hulk had its own kind of magnificence — and found it was the aft-end of the *Corfu Island,* wrecked here in 1963. Thirty years later, there were workers on it, salvaging metal with cutting torches, as if cutting up a great carcass. The men were like ants on this carcass; the ship was huge; and yet look what the sea did to it: turned it into a massive rusted monument to the Sublime. Look on it and feel scared. It's probably good for you.

Later I meet a woman who tells me that she has friends who come every year to the Magdalen Islands to "rest their souls." Seems possible; seems like a good idea.

Where to Stay

The first thing you want to do is pick up the current Tourist Guide to Îles de la Madeleine (available in English or French) at the tourist bureau at the end of the ferry dock (at rue Principal) in Cap-aux-Meules. This is the best tourist guide I have ever seen: it has very good maps to all of the islands, as well as history, and information about activities. Moreover, it lists all of the campgrounds and ho-tels/motels on the islands.

There are two kinds of private campgrounds in Québec, and there are two kinds of private campgrounds in Îles de la Madeleine. One kind emulates a lively little town; it can even have a nightclub. The other is more familiar to campers from English Canada: it provides the usual facilities (hot showers, flush toilets, electrical hook-ups), and suggests the rustic pleasures of outdoor living in the wilderness. I prefer the latter, and therefore recommend two campgrounds in Îles de la Madeleine.

The campground nearest the ferry dock — which you will prob-ably want if you have left your vehicle in Souris, Prince Edward Island, and come to the Magdalen Islands with tent and bicycle — is Camping Gros-Cap on Île du Cap aux Meules. You might want to stay here even if you have a vehicle, because the ferry docks at 7 p.m. and Camping Gros-Cap is handy for the first night. To get to Camp-ing Gros-Cap you leave the ferry dock and turn left on Chemin Principal at the tourist bureau. Continue for a few blocks, turn left on Chemin de Gros-Cap (it is marked), and ride or drive in a southerly direction for 5 km (3 mi) until you reach Chemin du Camping (marked), which takes you to the site of a one-time Fisheries Laboratory,

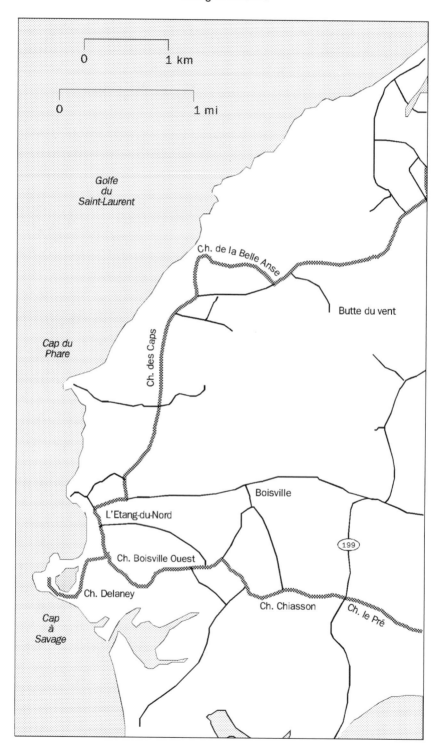

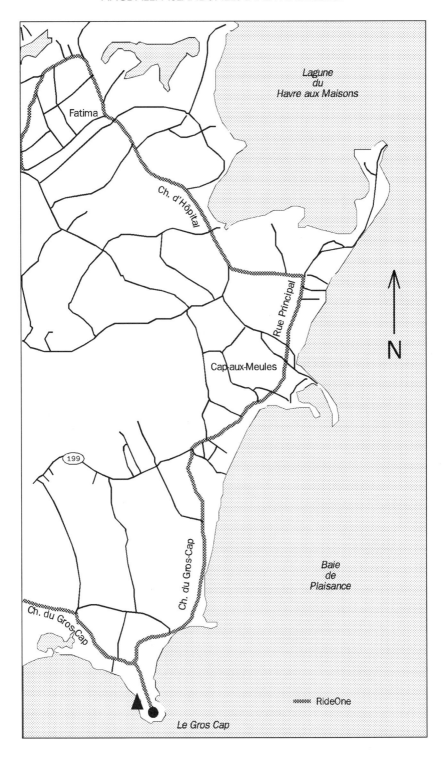

Lagune du Havre aux Maisons

Fatima

Ch. d'Hôpital

Rue Principal

Cap-aux-Meules

199

Ch. du Gros-Cap

Ch. du Gros-Cap

Baie de Plaisance

N

Le Gros Cap

RideOne

which is the location of Camping Gros-Cap. You will find the people friendly and helpful — but you will probably need whatever French you possess. *Camping Gros-Cap, Île du Cap aux Meules, G0B 1E0; (418) 986-4515*

Camping Gros-Cap is next to the sea, but well above the breaking waves, and it has the cyclists' necessities: hot showers, flush toilets — and laundry facilities as well. You will probably see other cyclists in their various gear.

We spent more time at Camping Plage du Golfe (and yes, *golfe* means *gulf*, not *golf*) simply because we liked it so much, and it was as handy as anywhere else to anywhere on the islands. You find Camping Plage du Golfe by driving south from Cap-aux-Meules on Québec 199 along the dune (windsurfers to your right on the broad enclosed waters) to Île du Hâvre Aubert, where you will see a large sign directing you to a right turn on Chemin du Bassin. Follow Chemin du Bassin to Camping Plage du Golfe. Camping Plage du Golfe has hot showers, flush toilets, laundry facilities — and ice. It is located on a lovely long beach. Ms. Luxe tells me that on Saturday night the girls gather in the washroom and spend hours applying elaborate make-up. *Camping Plage du Golfe, Chemin du Bassin, Île du Havre Aubert G0B 1A0; (418) 937-5224*

There are 16 hotels listed for the islands in the Tourist Guide. The Tourist Guide will give you Québec ratings and rates. The two which attracted me are among the more expensive, and both in Cap-aux-Meules: *Hôtel Château Madelinot, Route 199, C.P. 44 Cap-aux-Meules, G0B 1B0; (418) 986-3695;* or *Auberge Madeli, Rue Principale, Cape-aux-Meules, C.P. 427 G0B 1B0; (418) 986-2211.* The Tourist Guide lists a reservation service number: (418) 986-2245.

The Rides
Ride One: Île du Cap aux Meules
This ride is suitable for all kinds of bicycles.

It begins at Camping Gros-Cap. Ride out Chemin du Camping from the campground, and turn right on Chemin de Gros-Cap and ride back to Cap-aux-Meules, and turn right on Chemin Principal and pass by the tourist bureau and the road to the ferry dock and keep going straight up the hill on Chemin Principal and down the hill until you come to Chateau Madelinot. Here you turn left. The road is Chemin des Caps, but for some reason had no sign the day I was there. So turn left at Chateau Madelinot. Keep the sea on your right, stay on Chemin des Caps until you come to Chemin d'Hôpital, and follow it. It is, or was, marked. It will bend around past a sports complex with a waterslide (another campground is here, Le Barachois), but you will stay with Chemin d'Hôpital until you find yourself in the centre of the community of Fatima. Here you turn right in front of the Esso station. On the left corner of the intersection is École du Stella Maris. You are now on Chemin de Caps in a southerly direction. Stay on this road until you see, on your right, Chemin de la Belle Anse. Turn right. You'll know where to stop for the view. Rest and take it in, and be careful of the cliffs. Red sandstone, some of it cut away in chunks which might suggest Henry Moore. Continue on Chemin de la Belle Anse, which rejoins Chemin des Caps a bit farther on, and continue until you come to a T, just outside L'Étang-du-Nord. Turn right and cycle into L'Étang-du-Nord.

L'Étang-du-Nord is a busy, prosperous little fishing port, and there is a pleasant public park with a handy (good) casse-croute nearby for hot dogs or ice cream, and a large piece of concrete work-sculpture of fishermen hauling on a line. Look out to sea and you'll see seagulls howling after a boat coming into harbour. They follow the boat like flies after a garbage truck and then, when the boat enters the harbour, they stay outside. Odd. One of life's mysteries. Turn your gaze to your left, to the southwest, and you'll see the hulk of the *Corfu Island.* You can cycle to the beached wreck by taking Chemin Delaney across the bar and cycling up the hill. All right, you'll have to walk the last couple of hundred yards.

You leave L'Étang-du-Nord on Chemin Boisville Ouest (to which you return from viewing the hulk), and continue on Chemin Boisville Ouest in a southeasterly direction until you turn right on Chemin Chiasson. It will take you to Québec 199. Cross the highway and continue straight on Chemin Le Pré past some prosperous houses until you come to Chemin Gros-Cap. Turn right. (You may feel uneasy that you do not recognize any houses, and think that you began the ride on a road with this name. You did; but this is a different part of the road with the same name. Never mind. It will take you back to Chemin Camping.) At Chemin Camping turn right and cycle back to the campground.

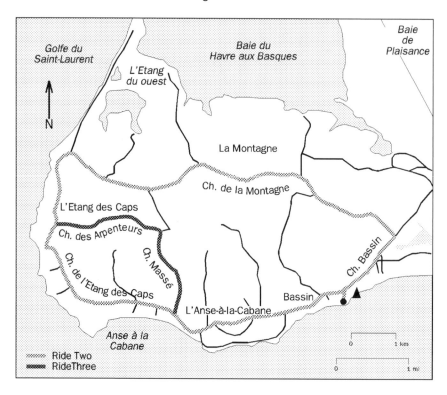

Ride Two: Île du Hâvre Aubert

Île du Havre Aubert is the southernmost island of the archipelago. You reach it via Québec 199. Camping Plage du Golfe is on Chemin du Bassin.

This ride is suitable for all kinds of bicycles.

The campground is on the shore, and to return to the road (Chemin du Bassin) is a goodly uphill pull out of the campground. Turn left at the top and follow Chemin du Bassin in a westerly direction. You'll see a lighthouse off to your left. Continue on and the road becomes Chemin de L'Étang des Caps. Stay on it and it becomes Chemin de la Montagne, which meets Chemin du Bassin. Turn right on Chemin du Bassin, and in very little time you are back at the campground.

What did you see? Tethered sheep, for one thing, and a couple of cows on a hillside for another. There is obviously some farming on this particular island. Barns are strangely absent — or not so strangely. You might see the ingenious *baraque,* which may demonstrate why there are no barns. The *baraque* is a clever structure for storing hay. It is four poles with a roof on ropes which is held up by the hay inside and slides down as the hay is taken out.

Ride Three: Île du Havre Aubert

This ride requires a mountain bicycle. It also begins at Camping Plage du Golfe.

Heave yourself up out of the campground and turn left at the top on Chemin du Bassin and zing along until you come to Chemin Massé, on your right. Turn right uphill on Chemin Massé and climb to the top past the gravel pit.

Stop here and look around. Some view! An exceptional vantage point to consider yourself in the universe. You might feel you have achieved a point of balance. Then back on your pedals and hang on to your brakes going down the other side.

Going down the other side you find yourself in a secluded valley where the bovine creatures have not seen your like before and the youngsters canter about in excitement and confusion. Guernseys, I believe.

This is a gravel road to the bottom of the hill, and at the bottom there is a crossroad. Turn left on it; it is a rough old road called Chemin des Arpenteurs. It is chiefly a dirt track. You will note the island's automobile graveyard to your right. Bounce along the dirt track of Chemin des Arpenteurs until it becomes pavement and meets Chemin de L'Étang des Caps — as it is called here. Turn left (southerly) and heave your way up the hills back to the campground — perhaps with some difficulty, if you encounter the winds I did. A challenge, those winds. When you find yourself pedalling downhill you know the wind is stiff; when you find yourself downshifting while pedalling downhill you know you have met one of nature's mundane challenges. Brings you back to earth, that wind does.

Ride Four: Île du Havre aux Maisons

You will want a mountain bike for this ride.

If you want a good 37 km (23 mi), you might want to start from Camping Gros Cap on Île du Cap aux Meules. Île du Havre aux Maisons is the island just north of Île du Cap aux Meules. But, as it happened, I drove my van to Île du Havre aux Maisons on Québec 199 and started the cycle ride from the picnic park on Chemin de la Dune du Sud. It's a lovely little park, with washrooms with sinks where you can fill up your water bottles, and flush toilets. There is a little

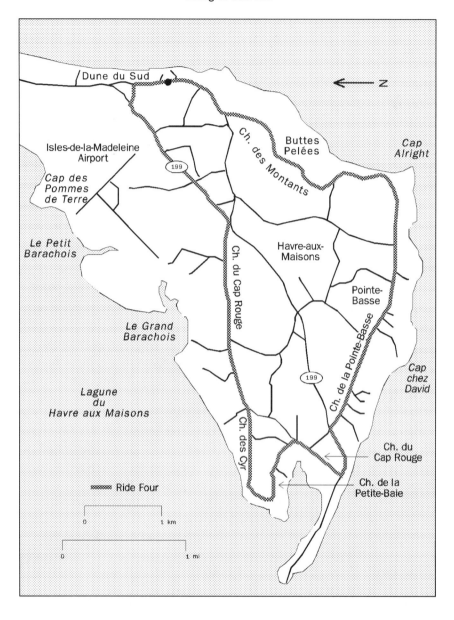

beach which is featured on many postcards. There is a sandstone arch, and you can stand under it, naturally framed, and have somebody take your photograph. In the background will be the sea and perhaps a bobbing fishing boat.

Leave the picnic park and turn left, uphill, southerly, on Chemin Dune du Sud to Chemin des Montants, where you turn left and climb the gravel road. At the top hang on to your brakes and fall through space into the shadows of the valley and partake of its curves past the farmhouse to the T with Chemin des Echouries. Turn left. Follow the road up another hill past the lighthouse; stop at the top and look back at the cliffs; feel awe and insignificance and continue on. The road acquires houses and becomes Chemin de la Point-Basse. You ride this until it meets Québec 199, where you turn left and pass Hotel Vieux Couvent on your left and Motel des Îles on your right, and Le P'tit Café, which seems to be very popular. Next to the restaurant is the Irving station at Chemin du Cap Rouge. Turn right on Chemin du Cap Rouge and follow it until you come to Chemin de la Petite Baie, where you turn left, and follow it until you are about to leap into the sea, where you turn right onto Chemin des Cyr. Stay on Chemin des Cyr, bearing left, until you find yourself again meeting Chemin du Cap Rouge, where you turn left, and continue to Québec 199, where you turn left again. You may notice planes whirring in to land at the airport; the airport of the Magdalen Islands is to your left. You will pass the Motel Theriault on your left, and, a little farther on, you will come to Chemin de la Dune du Sud, where you will turn right and return to the picnic park for further photographic sessions, if desired.

NOVA SCOTIA

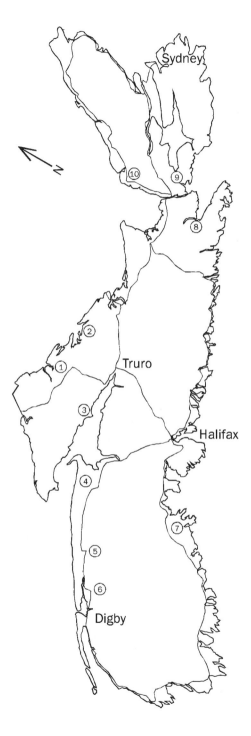

1. Pugwash and Wallace
2. Tatamagouche
3. Great Village
4. Wolfville and Kentville
5. Bridgetown
6. Annapolis Royal
7. Lunenburg
8. Guysborough
9. Isle Madame
10. Mabou

PUGWASH and WALLACE

DISTANCE: 45 km (28 mi), including 8 km (5 mi) diversion to Fox Harbour Park **TIME:** 2 hrs 30 min	**DIFFICULTY:** Moderate **OTHER FACTORS:** Wind, one steep hill.

Big Thinkers

It is always yesterday that there were giants in the land. Not now. It seems that you always have to look back at least a hundred years ago. But you can see evidence of these giants of industry and commerce in surprising corners of the Maritimes. Lord Beaverbrook (actually a short little fellow) is clearly evident in Fredericton, New Brunswick, and the Scottish-born American oil millionaire Alexander McDonald lives on in memory in his fine summer residence at Dalvay, Prince Edward Island.

In Pugwash, Nova Scotia, you can roam the streets and roads where Cyrus Eaton grew up to become an American steel magnate, financier, and head of the Chesapeake and Ohio Railroad before he returned home with his *largesse* and his ideas.

Eaton was like Andrew Carnegie, in that he believed in the value of thrift and hard work (Pugwash is Scottish, of course, so Scottish that the street signs are in Gaelic as well as English), but Eaton also believed (as did Carnegie) in ideas. Eaton sponsored and hosted the early Pugwash Thinkers' Conferences, which began in 1955 at the instigation of the old British radical, Bertrand Russell, seconded by Albert Einstein. The conferences brought scientists from behind the Iron Curtain to Pugwash to talk with scientists from Europe and North America. The place was awash in ideas — and, some say, in controversy. Eaton received the Lenin Peace Prize in 1960. *That* set some tongues to wagging — chiefly in the United States, where Eaton had lived since 1900. He had become a U.S. citizen in 1913, after completing his studies at McMaster University and deciding not to go into the Protestant ministry. The famous Thinkers' Conferences were held in different places in the world (although often designated as "Pugwash Conferences") on an irregular basis for a time, but there have been none recently. The Eaton Foundation still hosts an occasional Pugwash conference on one topic or another at the Eaton summer residence.

Every year in Pugwash there is now a gathering of the Scottish clans. They meet in Eaton Park, on the waterfront. Each year a different clan is featured. You can revel in tartan if you choose.

But, for me, the ride from Wallace in a loop through Pugwash and back was less a pursuit of Eaton's controversial ideals and millions than it was the quiet contemplation of the ice floes still drifting in the Northumberland Strait (it was the middle of May) and the tombstone (1881) of Reverend Munro at the Melville United Church. I was contemplating notions of Eternity. I was thinking of seascapes, horizontal abstractions of colour, light, mood. Or — more like Eaton than I thought — I was considering the bigger picture.

But the smaller picture has its delights, too. There was a charming herd of nanny goats on this route. And in the Dutch Mill Motel Restaurant in Wallace, I was told about these guys from Halifax who come to Wallace every year to snare rabbits in the town dump. I liked the notion of sport in the town dump. The rabbits fetch a good price in the Halifax market. The fellows stay in the Dutch Mill Motel (where I was staying, too) and seek their fortunes in small as their ancestors did in large: by trapping. I admit, however, that the new fellows' endeavours lack something in dimension. There are no longer giants in the land.

Where to Stay

There is a private campground, Gulf Shores Camping Park, 11 km (7 mi) from Pugwash off Route 6 on the Gulf Shore Road — on the loop, therefore. It looked right pleasant from the road, but in the middle of May it was not yet open. In the Nova Scotia guide to accommodations the open dates are given as June 27 through September 7. It has showers and washrooms and offers swimming and a putting green. It is handy, in fact, to a golf course just down the road a piece. *Gulf Shore Camping Park, Gulf Shore Road, Pugwash, Nova Scotia B0K 1L0; (902) 243-2489.*

Or you might want to consider the Blue Heron Inn, which comes highly recommended by friends. It is open from June 10 through Labour Day, and has 5 bedrooms, two with private bath, two with a shared bath, and one with a half-bath. A continental breakfast is provided. *Blue Heron Inn, Durham Street, Box 405, Pugwash, Nova Scotia B0K 1L0; (902) 243-2900; (winter) (902) 243-2516.*

But Ms. Luxe and I stayed at the Dutch Mill Motel and Restaurant, which was more my kind of place than hers but comfy in a rustic sort of way, and spotless. You can recognize it (surprise!) by the windmill. It is the kind of place where the restaurant features liver & onions. I like liver & onions. Generous helpings. A cyclist needs generous helpings. The music in the restaurant is not exactly in the background and features country songs and gospel. I like country songs and gospel. Ms. Luxe was certainly understanding. The Dutch Mill Motel is open from April 1 through January 1. Reasonable rates. *Dutch Mill Motel and Restaurant, R.R. #1, Wallace, Nova Scotia B0K 1Y0; (902) 257-2598.*

The Ride

The ride can of course begin anywhere on the loop, but I began at Wallace, from the Dutch Mill Motel. A couple of hundred metres beyond the motel toward Wallace you turn left and cross a small bridge. You are riding in a northerly direction. Some 4 km (2.5 mi) along the road you will see a sign which tells you that if you turn right on the dirt road you will come to Fox Harbour (picnic) Park. This is an 8 km (5 mi) diversion. It is a pleasant little park with boardwalks out onto the mudflats. Return to the paved road. Turn right; continue northward. The road is breaking-up macadam, somewhere between asphalt and chipseal. When you are near the shore the road turns left and west and you are on the Gulf Shore Road which runs past the Gulf Shore Camping Park and the golf course. Near Pugwash there is another picnic park, and then you sail downhill (south) on the Shore Road into Pugwash and meet Route 6 at the Pizza Delight. Turn left and east on Route 6 — careful, there is some traffic — and return to Wallace. There is one low-gear hill between Pugwash and Wallace on Route 6.

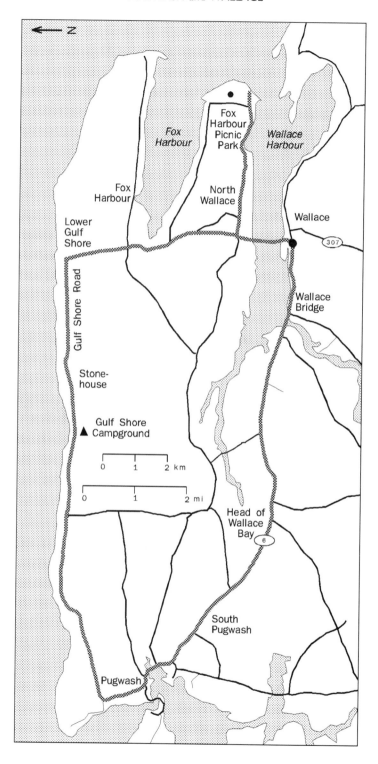

Fox Harbour

Fox Harbour Picnic Park

Wallace Harbour

Fox Harbour

North Wallace

Wallace

Lower Gulf Shore

307

Gulf Shore Road

Wallace Bridge

Stone-house

▲ Gulf Shore Campground

0   1   2 km

0   1   2 mi

Head of Wallace Bay

6

South Pugwash

Pugwash

The Great Yellow Dog of Pugwash

I caught a glimpse of him out of the corner of my eye as I was leaving Pugwash on Route 6. Perhaps I heard a child cry out, "Come back!" When I looked around I saw him far back in the distance: a big yellow dog running flat out. But I was going downhill in top gear and was away ahead of him. Besides, usually a dog gets tired or bored in less than a hundred yards, and I had easily three hundred yards on him.

But then there was a little rise in the road and I had to downshift, and when I looked around, he was still coming: running flat out, gaining. He was close enough so I could see his red tongue hanging out of his mouth and recognize that this was a Big Yellow Dog. But not to worry: now I was going downhill again, and besides, I had a can of dog mace (of dubious legality) handy. Anyway, I had a lead of at least a quarter mile on him. However, when I stole a glance behind, he was still coming. He was running in the centre of the road. He could easily get hit by a car. I wished him no ill; I am fond of dogs; but I was becoming suspicious of this beast. He was persistent, and he was gaining — and there, ahead of me, was a hill. The only hill on this route. It was a hill which was going to require granny-gears, and the Great Yellow Dog of Pugwash was gaining.

The usual advice in these situations, which is usually good, is to get off your bike and keep it between you and the beast, and hope that somebody comes along to call him off or he gets bored and goes home. I was considering that. I was considering my ancestral snarl. I come from generations of rural men who, no matter how fond they are of their dogs, have no hesitation in snarling "Git, git, *git!*" at any and all dogs when they are underfoot. You keep the damned dogs in their damned place! The sound I make is a sound I hear from me at no other time — and it usually works. The dog recognizes the sound of a man who will pull his damned tail out through his mouth if he's not careful. I was ready to speak harshly to the Great Yellow Dog of Pugwash.

And the crisis point, the hill, was there ahead of me. I was down in granny-gear one, and he was at my back wheel and I was preparing for combat — when he shot by me in a burst of Triumph and was up the hill in Joy. The damned beast was not chasing me; he was racing me.

He won. He was delighted with himself. You could almost see him raising his paws in Victory.

There's a moral here. You probably can't outrun a determined dog. And all the dogs in the neighbourhood, who were properly tied, were giving the Great Yellow Dog hell for his adolescent heedless behaviour. But all of a sudden I was fond of him. I told him to get over to the side of the road before he got hit by a car and killed. I told him he was a good dog but he should go home. I told him I'd adopt him but he belonged to that kid back there and besides, he was very dirty — he'd clearly been hanging out in the tidal flats and was black with mud up his belly — and I didn't think I could get him into the shower at the Dutch Mill Motel, and besides, Ms. Luxe would have him sleeping at her feet in moments, and how would he like that? She'd make a house pet of him, so if he had any regard for his future, he'd better go home, and he did.

TATAMAGOUCHE

Ride One	Ride Two
DISTANCE: 36 km (22 mi)	**DISTANCE:** 51 km (32 mi)
TIME: 2 hrs	**TIME:** 2 hrs 30 min
DIFFICULTY: Moderate	**DIFFICULTY:** Moderate
OTHER FACTORS: The use of the rail-trail requires a mountain bike and more energy than using the paved roads — but there are no major hills on these routes.	

By Bicycle to Denmark

What does it tell you about a small town that it has a good dime store and no parking meters? Tatamagouche has a good dime store, a couple of handy eateries, a supermarket, two museums, a laundromat, no parking meters, and the Train Station Inn. More about the Train Station Inn in a moment. Right now I'm in the dime store, exulting in the old familiar smell of sweeping compound, textiles, and cheap chocolate candy. But what I purchase here is some green household cleaner which is advertised as "biodegradable," which I am willing to believe, which was recommended to me by Peter Williams of Sussex, New Brunswick, as the best stuff ever to get the guck off your chain. Turns out he's right. I use a dish brush to get into the links.

There are also good ice cream cones handy on the main street.

There is an old creamery in Tatamagouche, down by the tracks, which no longer operates, but if you listen closely you can hear the rattle of milk cans in your memory. My grandfather used to take me in his Model A truck (he kept it in the barn; it was covered with dust and bits of straw) down to the creamery to deliver the milk. That was in another place, of course, a long time ago. It was the high point of the summer morning for the city kid on a summer visit.

In the Fraser Cultural Centre, which is down the street there a piece, you can see the dress worn by Anna Swan, who was born in nearby New Annan in 1846 and grew to be 7 feet 11 inches tall, and weighed 413 pounds. It is a very big dress. She was exhibited by Phineas T. Barnum, and in 1870 she married another giant, Captain Van Buren Bates of Kentucky, with whom she toured the world and visited Queen Victoria. She and Bates had two children, a daughter and a son who, at 23 pounds, is believed to be the largest live birth ever recorded — but both children died quickly. These are important facts in a rural neighbourhood. You can read about Anna Swan in Phyllis R. Blakeley's *Two Remarkable Giants* (the other is not Bates, but Angus McAskill from Cape Breton), which you can purchase at the Fraser Cultural Centre, as I did. There is also a recent novel about Anna Swan, but it is terrible and best avoided, and if encountered, forgotten. I've forgotten its title.

The last passenger train came through Tatamagouche in 1963, and the last freight rumbled through in 1973. The old station was virtually abandoned, but local entrepreneur Jim LeFresne acquired it and turned it into the noteworthy Train Station Inn, which is a favourite overnight stop for cyclists from everywhere and the occasional celebrity like the Governor-General of Canada, who came here on one locally famous occasion to escape from his hand-shaking duties. It was a private visit, and therefore no one in town was supposed to know. Everyone in town agreed they didn't know he was here. Pictures are available.

Cyclists are especially fond of the Train Station Inn because the proprietor has thoughtfully provided a kitchenette, where you can prepare your own snacks late into the night, and laundry facilities. You can sit out on the deck (as I did) and gaze down the path where the tracks used to be and plan your next day's ride.

The Train Station Inn utilizes what were once the stationmaster's quarters as its inn facilities. You will sleep in a bedroom full of antiques, and in the evening you may sit in the stationmaster's lounge and, as in the old days, peruse the photograph album, and talk with the other travellers of where you have been and where you are going. We talked of Saint John, New Brunswick, and Îles de la Madeleine. Everyone has a story, and it is amazing the number of places people have been.

The next morning you will (likely) stock up on carbohydrates in the form of blueberry pancakes (I did; delicious!) and take up the rail-trail for one of the most interesting rides in the Maritimes.

Where to Stay

There is a good simple municipal campground at Tatamagouche with shade, flush toilets, and free hot showers. It is right on Route 6, 2 km (1 mi) west of Tatamagouche, and is open from May 15 through September 15. *Nelson Memorial Park and Campground, R.R. #3, Tatamagouche, Nova Scotia B0K 1V0; (902) 657-2730.*

The Train Station Inn is open year round, and has 4 rooms with private bath/shower and a TV in the lounge with VHS. Reservations are recommended. *The Train Station Inn, Station Road, Box 67, Tatamagouche, Nova Scotia B0K 1V0; (902) 657-3222.*

Ride One

You will need a mountain bike if you use the rail-trail. If you have a ten-speed, you can adapt the route to use only paved roads.

It feels like a great idea to leave from the station and cycle directly into the bush, but it would be a good idea to think twice. The old rail roadbed just at the station was "improved" in its last active days by the addition of big river gravel — which is impossible to cycle through. All right, don't believe me: try it.

Start your ride the other side of the highway (Route 6) beyond the railway bridge, down the old railbed in an easterly direction. Most of the railbed was created by dumping cinders from the old coal-fired steam locomotives, and the cinders have made an excellent cycling path. At about 6.5 km (4 mi) and 10 km (6 mi) you will find some patches of fat gravel, but you can ride through them. You follow the old railbed to the point where it crosses Route 326 at a community called Denmark (which has nothing whatever to do with the Scandinavian country) where you will see, on your left, the Sutherland Steam Mill, which is operated by the province of Nova Scotia as a museum. It is worth a visit.

(The alternative route for ten-speed bicycles is this: leave Tatamagouche on Route 311 south and just outside of town, turn left [east] on the Middleton to River John Road [it is marked] and ride to the junction with Route 326 near the community of Denmark. You have been riding roughly parallel to the old rail-line.)

Turn right (southerly) on Route 326 through the gathering of houses known as Denmark, and continue until you come to the clearly marked junction with Route 256, which is also known as the Balmoral Road. You will probably see a sign directing you along this road to the Balmoral Grist Mill, which is also a Nova Scotia provincial museum. Turn right (westerly) on Route 256 and ride to the Balmoral Grist Mill, where you might wish to fill your water bottle (I did) at Archie's Well. Continue west on Route 256 until it meets Route 311. Turn right (north) on Route 311 and follow it back to Tatamagouche. You will have ridden approximately 36 km (22 mi).

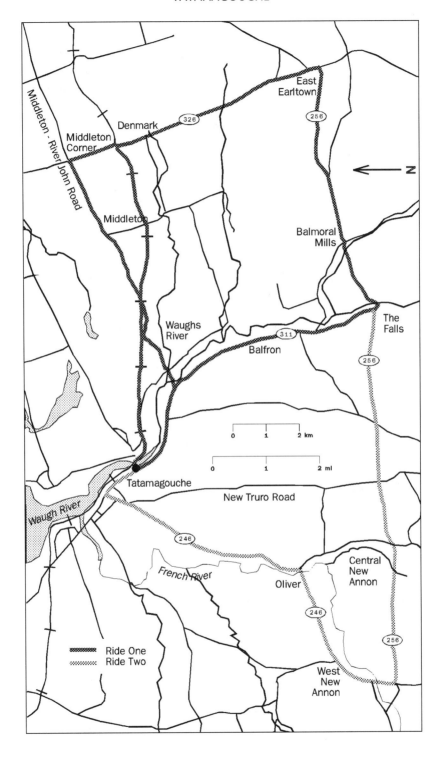

East
Earltown

Denmark

326

256

Middleton
Corner

N

Middleton-RiverJohn Road

Middleton

Balmoral
Mills

The
Falls

Waughs
River

311

256

Balfron

0   1   2 km

0   1   2 ml

Tatamagouche

New Truro Road

Waugh River

246

French River

Oliver

Central
New
Annon

246

256

Ride One
Ride Two

West
New
Annon

Ride Two

An extended ride can be achieved by staying on Route 256, crossing Route 311, and continuing on through Central New Annan — Anna Swan country — to the junction with Route 246. Note the digits. Turn right (north) on Route 246, and return to Tatamagouche. You will have added approximately 15 km (9 mi) to the loop.

Big Deer, Little Bell

I was cycling out of Tatamagouche on the old rail-line at a pretty good clip — probably going as fast as the train ever did, about 20 km/hr — when I happened upon a deer in the roadway ahead. I rang my bell.

I have a bell on my bicycle. I bought it at the local Canadian Tire store; it is decorated with a little Canadian flag. It was the bell available when I decided I needed a bell. A bell is useful on a bicycle. It is also almost always required by law everywhere (from the old days), but no one anywhere ever pays any attention to that. But I learned the value of a bell when I was cycling in Denmark, where cyclists overtake one another with a cheerful little ringing and a friendly nod and a "Good day" (in Danish). So I bought a bell when I returned, and now, when I approach pedestrians on the road or along a shared path (they are almost invariably lost in their thoughts of the wonders of nature or the cares of society), I ring my little bell and they do not jump out of their skins as I pass. It makes for good relations. They frequently thank me for my courteous little bell.

So I have a little bell on my mountain bike which goes ting-a-ling.

Approaching the deer, who was grazing in the roadbed, I rang my little bell: ting-a-ling.

The deer did not look up.

I rang again. Ting-a-ling. I was closing rapidly on the fellow. This was a big fellow. Bigger than I was on the bicycle. Ting-a-ling.

The deer raised his head, glanced around, met my eyes. The deer's eyes spoke clearly: "Do you mind?" they said. "I'm having my lunch here."

And the deer returned to grazing. The deer in these parts do not unsettle easily.

Ting-a-ling! Ting-a-ling!

Again the deer glanced around.

The deer had a big white tail at my eye level.

Ting-a-ling!!!

You have to admit that I made a pretty sight: helmet, glasses, beard, on two wheels, bearing down, closing fast, ting-a-ling, ting-a-ling!

Deer, it is clear, are not necessarily quick-witted in the wilderness, but at last the image of me struck his brain — struck it, I venture to say, a blow of astonishment.

He leapt straight up in the air and hit the ground running, and I was hot on his heels, thundering down the railbed, *ting-a-ling, ting-a-ling, ting-a-ling!*

GREAT VILLAGE

Ride One	Ride Two
DISTANCE: 23 km (14 mi)	**DISTANCE:** 38 km (23 mi)
TIME: 1 hr 20 min	**TIME:** 2 hrs
DIFFICULTY: Moderate	**DIFFICULTY:** Moderate
OTHER FACTORS: None	**OTHER FACTORS:** Rough dirt road

Elizabeth Bishop

Scholars are curious people. Pun intended. One friend of mine, who writes articles and delivers papers on the work of the American poet and prose writer Elizabeth Bishop, is also a devout fly-fisherman, and he says that he has every intention of fishing the streams around Great Village just because Uncle Neddy did. My friend says proudly that he has held Uncle Neddy's fly-rod in his hand.

I am no scholar, but I'm also a curious fellow. Pun intended. And I am cycling around Great Village because of Elizabeth Bishop, and it doesn't take me long to figure out how Uncle Neddy might have conveniently acquired his booze. Elizabeth Bishop seems a little puzzled on this point. She notes that the nearest government liquor store was fifteen miles away. "Probably when Uncle Neddy went to town he brought back a supply of rum, the usual drink, heavy, dark, and strong." But the train at Londonderry Station was only five miles away, and, if he'd had a bicycle (did he? we don't know), he could have been at the station in less than half an hour. Then, too, the bootlegger has been an institution in the Maritimes for many, many years.

Elizabeth Bishop, the prize-winning American poet and prosewriter, spent an important part of her youth in Great Village, and she wrote about Great Village out of all proportion to the time she spent here. Mind you, it was a very significant time for her; a terrible time for her. She was a little girl in the home of her grandparents — just across from the Presbyterian church, next to the General Store — when her mother screamed one afternoon and went irrevocably mad. Elizabeth Bishop writes about it in the story, "In the Village," which appeared in *The New Yorker* in December 1953, and which you can find in her *Collected Prose*. The story begins with the church steeple.

A scream, the echo of a scream, hangs over that Nova Scotia village. No one hears it; it hangs there forever, a slight stain in those pure blue skies, skies that travelers compare to those of Switzerland, too dark, too blue, so that they seem to keep on darkening a little more around the horizon—or is it around the rims of the eyes? — the color of the cloud of bloom on the elm trees, the violet on the fields of oats; something darkening over the woods and waters as well as the sky. The scream hangs like that, unheard, in memory — in the past, in the present, and those years between. It was not even loud to begin with, perhaps. It just came there to live, forever — not loud, just alive forever. Its pitch would be the pitch of my village. Flick the lightning rod on top of the church steeple with your fingernail and you will hear it.

A wrought-iron owl has replaced the lightning rod.

Uncle Neddy — as he is named in "Memories of Uncle Neddy" — also lived across from the Presbyterian church, but opposite the General Store, on the other corner. His house was for sale the day I was there. Uncle Neddy, in Elizabeth Bishop's account, was the sometimes charming black devil, the evil Santa Claus: a tinsmith, a fly-fisherman, a drunk.

Through this village the little girl drove Nelly the Jersey cow; here she nodded "Good day" to the clergyman in the black straw hat while Nelly plopped unconcerned. Later in the story the girl will stop on the bridge to stare down at the river (as you will, too; it is very difficult not to stop on a bridge to stare down at the water) at "all the little trout that have been too smart to get caught — for how long now?" She will also take the weekly package, from her grandmother to her mother in the asylum, to the post office, and find to her shame that the parcel is too big to fit through the wicket, and therefore must be handed into the building through an outside window. You can go to the post office and see the same wicket — but the building is a different one now, although much the same. This one would do perfectly for the movie.

I came to idle about the village in Elizabeth Bishop's mind and look at things through her eyes. The village seemed bigger to her, of course; she was writing from the point of view of a little girl. I look from the grandparents' house toward the Presbyterian church where the little girl imagined her friend Gwendolyn Appletree's coffin

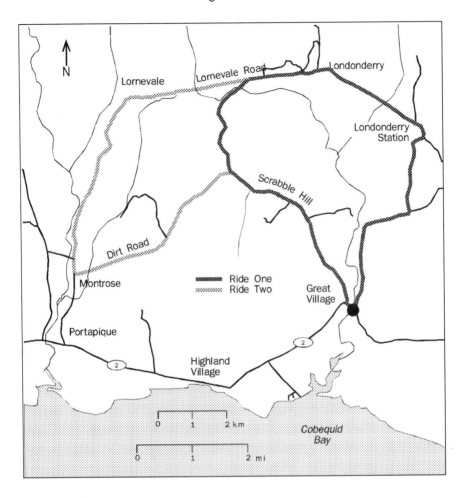

propped up against the church doors. You can go out to the graveyard to see Gwendolyn Patriquin's grave; I did. She is given the name Appletree in the story.

I cycled past the cenotaph ("I wanted us to win the war but I didn't want to be an American") and past the Baptist church ("The Baptism") and up to Londonderry ("Galway Mines" in the fiction), where Aunt Hat, Uncle Neddy's fierce wife, came from. Tales were told about the origin of her red hair and the red-haired priest of Londonderry — which once was an iron-mining town of some five thousand people, with its own blast furnaces and rolling mill. Now it is a gathering of houses. There is a little museum there which is well worth the visit. Violent deaths in dangerous work; a flood; a confrontation between striking workers and the mine manager's son. I rode past the Roman Catholic church and across the hills and down Scrabble Hill and back to Great Village, where the scholars are already setting up shop. You might find one or two of them nosing about with notebooks and cameras. You might mistake one of them for me.

Where to Stay

There are no accommodations in or especially handy to Great Village.

Hidden Hilltop Park, on Route 102 north of Glenholme, is an adequate private campground with the required facilities: showers and flush toilets. It is approximately 10 km (6 mi) from Great Village. I have stayed here; it's OK. The season is 1 May through 15 October. *Hidden Hilltop Park, R.R. #1, Debert, Nova Scotia B0M 1G0; (902) 662-3391, (902) 895-8055.*

I have also stayed at the privately owned and operated Masstowner Motel, just at Exit 12 of Route 104, some 5 km (3 mi) from Great Village. It provides simple, clean, more-than-adequate accommodation, and friendly people. I recommend it. There is an attached licensed dining room; the rates are reasonable. However, *do not plan to cycle from here to Great Village*; the road is too dangerous. *Masstowner Motel, R.R. #1, Debert, Nova Scotia B0M 1G0; (902) 662-2500.*

Ride One

You will want a mountain bike for this ride, although a hybrid might be adequate. Not recommended for ten-speed bikes.

This ride takes you from a rural village, past good farms, to the remnants of a nineteenth century industrial mining village, through some bush, and back to the rural village.

This ride begins at the cenotaph and uses the Londonderry Road. Therefore I parked my van in the parking lot of the Faith Baptist Church, which is just up the hill of the Londonderry Road past the cenotaph, and cycled northeast on the Londonderry Road to the first fork (at 3 km [2 mi]), where I took the left (west) branch to Londonderry Station, which is not now what it once was. The ride continues straight on to Londonderry, where it curves left (westerly) through the valley (ignore the possible turning at the Roman Catholic church) and up a granny-gear hill, where the surface becomes dirt and gravel. At the first turning left (south) there will be a sign which says Great Village, Great Village - Lornevale Rd; follow the arrow on the sign which directs you left, south, back down Scrabble Hill to Great Village. Ignore any possible turnings.

Ride Two

If you want a longer, somewhat more adventurous ride, continue straight at the Great Village turning (above) and continue on through Lornevale (I admit I did not notice a community here) and follow the road as it curves south to a place called Montrose, where a left turn (easterly) will take you along a rough dirt road back to Scrabble Hill, where you will turn right (southerly) and back to Great Village. I did not cycle this extended loop, but drove it in a vehicle. This will add approximately 15 km (9 mi) to the Great Village - Londonderry loop.

WOLFVILLE - KENTVILLE

DISTANCE: 50 km (31 mi)	**DIFFICULTY:** Easy to Moderate
TIME: 3 hrs	

Swanning & Lolling

I am lolling about at Victoria's Historic Inn in Wolfville, Nova Scotia. I fancy myself becoming rather good at lolling about. After all, there is a *chaise longue* in our room, and what can you do with a *chaise longue* but display yourself at your ease? I think I am beginning to get the hang of the loll.

And enjoying every minute of it, as is Ms. Luxe, who is in her element, swanning about among the rich furnishings, smiling. She can trail her hand artistically down the banister descending to dinner. We have the Seafood Coquille. I had a decent (enough) suit packed in the bottom of my duffel. I am wearing my most tweedy smile. My conversation is quick, decisive. "Haw!" I say, and "Haw!" again. Dispute that, if you will!

The wine is crisp — yes, thank you, quite acceptable. It will do nicely. Yes, we can grace these rooms. Nobody will know that back home we live in a house with aluminum siding.

No, I mean it. Ms Luxe is to this manner born, and I'm an actor: I can fake it quite convincingly. In no time at all we know in our hearts, souls, bones, that we belong in the tall Victorian rooms with their oval pictures on the wall (frequently of charming little rich children and attendant dogs), where the bathrooms feature soft heavy towels and there are baskets of flowers everywhere. All right, the flowers are made of silk, but they are real silk. I like it here. There is a writing desk in our room. No, I love it here. This is where the U.S.-based international cycling tours stay, and I am granting them no superiority whatever. I mean, they travel with vans trailing them to collect all the discarded sweat and probably the grunts, too. I belong here.

On the morrow we shall sally forth to view low tide on the Grand Pré, which is the title of a poem every Canadian schoolchild used to know, written by Bliss Carman (1861-1929), who was Edith Wharton's favourite poet for a while. It is not a bad poem at all. Here is my favorite stanza from it; note the subtle canoe imagery:

The while the river at our feet —
A drowsy inland meadow stream —
At set of sun the after-heat
Made running gold, and in the gleam
We freed our birch upon the stream.

Of course, the poem that gets great play in the international media is not Carman's but Henry Wadsworth Longfellow's *Evangeline*, which is one of those poems more talked about than read, and more referred to (knowingly, of course, with nods) than talked about. Here is the first stanza, which is one of those passages every American schoolchild used to know, in times primeval:

This is the forest primeval. The murmuring pines and the hemlocks,
Bearded with moss, and in garments green, indistinct in the twilight,
Stand like Druids of eld, with voices sad and prophetic,
Stand like harpers hoar, with beards that rest on their bosoms.
Loud from its rocky caverns, the deep-voiced neighboring ocean
Speaks, and in accents disconsolate answers the wail of the forest.

Uh-huh. You can just imagine the choked chortles evoked by those "harpers hoar," to say nothing of those old guys with beards resting on bosoms. I have just such a beard. And you are not going to find too many hemlocks bearded with moss in this clime, and I am not acquainted with any rocky caverns with deep voices. Longfellow did no field work. But this first stanza is nonetheless the best of the poem. It gets worse. Much worse.

But it does commemorate a terrible event. The French settlers (the Acadians) of the seventeenth century constructed the dykes here and lived in amity until 1755, when the British at Halifax became convinced that the Acadians were a threat to British hegemony (I love that word) in the area — and it is true that the Acadians refused to swear allegiance and fealty and that sort of thing to the British crown — so the Acadians were loaded on ships and sent forth to Louisiana to become Cajuns. In no time at all new settlers (from New England) came in to take up the vacant lands — which were, as noted, quite rich and productive. The richness of the lands probably had nothing to do with the earnestness of policy (it wouldn't have, would it?) — but the Expulsion of the Acadians is an event which still has an effect on the life of the Maritime provinces, as the Civil War lives on in the U.S. South, for example.

Longfellow's long narrative poem is the story of the expulsion.

Evangeline is a young woman whose wedding day is interrupted by the event. She and her groom-to-be, Gabriel, are put on separate ships and sent south to a different life in what became the United States. (Longfellow had a scarcely disguised political motive in telling this tale, as you might guess.) Evangeline wanders all over the continental U.S. looking for her Gabriel. At last she becomes a sister of mercy in a hospital in Philadelphia where she finds Gabriel — dying. He recognizes her just before he dies. It's a sad story. You can think about it while riding the roads nearby and across the dykes constructed by the Acadians in the seventeenth century.

In fact, I made two trips to this area — one with Ms. Luxe, which involved a good deal of lolling and swanning about in Wolfville, and another on my own (as Joe Spartan) in which I put up in a great little old-fashioned (1950s) motel in Kentville and rode out from there. You have your choice of ambience. And yes, there is a provincial campground near here, and it is one of the three provincial campgrounds in Nova Scotia with flush toilets and hot water, but it is (surprise, surprise) usually crammed to capacity, and is, moreover, out on the top of Blomidon with a great view from one of the most bodacious, humungous hills I ever hope to see, and no, we are not going to climb it by bicycle, are we? That's for the whippets on wheels. It is the kind of activity which leads to Pride, which leadeth to a Fall, and you and I are not going to risk theological insecurity, are we? You and I are here to take in the air, the sights, the good life in the common old-fashioned way — aren't we? (There is a Tim Horton's down the street in Wolfville; I'm going there for coffee and talk and muffins. Hey! This is the good life.)

Where to Stay

Forget about camping.

Allen's Motel in Kentville is 2 km (1 mi) west of the town centre in a residential section on Park Street. The prices are very reasonable; the rooms are spotless; they will have everything you need. The motel is operated by its owners, and a delicious set breakfast is available at a very reasonable price in the dining room next to the office. It is open all year round. It is my kind of place. NO credit cards, however. *Allen's Motel, 384 Park Street, Kentville, Nova Scotia B4N 1M9; (902) 678-2683.*

Victoria's Historic Inn and Motel is a four-star inn and registered historic property. It is a wonderful theatre in which to play at possessing old money and good breeding, unless of course you come by both naturally, in which case you will feel quite at home. Ms. Luxe and I enjoyed ourselves tremendously. The licensed dining room offers excellent cuisine. (Not just food, eh?) It is open the year round; it has honeymoon suites; a whirlpool bath is available. *Victoria's Historic Inn and Motel, 416 Main Street, Box 308, Wolfville, Nova Scotia B0P 1X0; (902) 542-5744.*

The Ride

You will probably want to use a hybrid or a mountain bike for this route. There is a short stretch of dirt road and a hybrid (at least) is necessary for the paths atop the dykes. I used a mountain bike, as always. This is, however, an unusually pleasant ride along good rural roads through orchard country, with dairy farms and at least one horse farm. You can see why the international cycling tours come here.

You can begin at either Kentville or Wolfville. I have made the entirely arbitrary decision to begin the description of the route in Kentville.

Find Belcher Street in Kentville. It is across the tracks at the light near the old station. Ride easterly on Belcher Street for approximately 10 km (6 mi) to the bridge in Port Williams. Turn right and cross the bridge, and if you have either a mountain bike or a hybrid, you can ride the dyke which snakes east across the marsh to Wolfville, a distance of approximately 6 km (4 mi). You will come into Wolfville by its old wharf and find yourself near Tim Horton's, where you can stop for a coffee and muffin. Then ride back through Wolfville in a westerly direction past Victoria's Historic Inn to Route 358 at the ubiquitous Irving station and turn right, northerly, back to Port Williams.

Follow Route 358 through Port Williams in a northerly direction until you come to Starr Point Road. There is a sign. (You will see this place designated as Starr Point, Starrs Point, and Starr's Point on one map or another. I've made an arbitrary decision.) Turn right (easterly) on Starr Point Road. Watch for signs to the historic Prescott House (built in 1814 by merchant and horticulturist Charles Ramage Prescott, who introduced better varieties of apple to the region), which you may or may not wish to visit. Our ride passes right by it. The road loops around Starr Point and intersects with the Wellington Dyke Road. Turn right. You will come to a T. Turn left, and then right again within 1 km (.5 mi) onto the dirt and gravel road which you follow to the T, and turn left on the pavement back to Route 358 at the Ultramar station. Turn right (northerly) on route 358 and ride to the village of Canning, where you will turn left (westerly) on Route 221 at the T — unless of course you want to ride into the village of

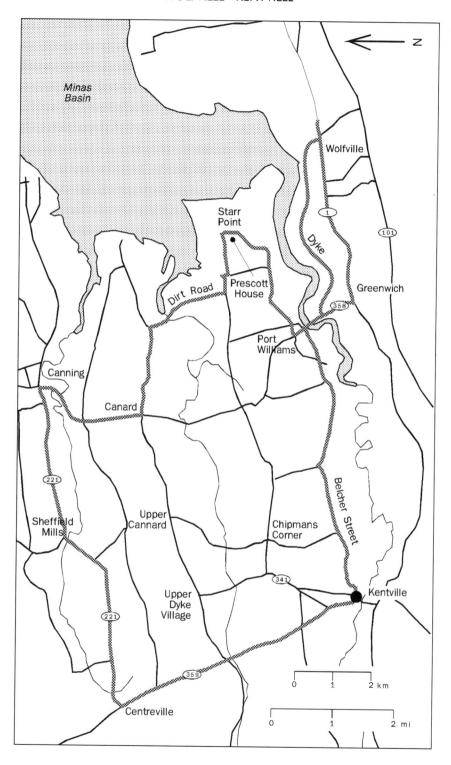

Minas
Basin

Wolfville

Starr
Point

Dyke

Prescott
House

Greenwich

Dirt Road

Port
Williams

Canning

Canard

Belcher Street

Sheffield
Mills

Upper
Cannard

Chipmans
Corner

Kentville

Upper
Dyke
Village

Centreville

0   1   2 km

0   1   2 mi

Canning, which has food and drink attractions and, in the centre, a monument to the local Boer War hero, Lt. Robert Borden. Back on the road on Route 221 west you will have a quick little turn in the gathering of houses known as Sheffield Mills (watch for that turn) as Route 221 continues west after a hiccup. You will ride through Gibson's Wood on this Route 221 until it comes to a T in Centreville at Route 359. Turn left (southerly) on Route 359 to Kentville.

BRIDGETOWN

DISTANCE: 33 km (20.5 mi)	**OTHER FACTORS:** Narrow
TIME: 1 hr 30 min	shoulder on Route 1.
DIFFICULTY: Easy	

The Rural Life

The writer Ernest Buckler lived here all his life — and recorded everything he saw meticulously and metaphorically in *The Mountain and the Valley* and *Ox Bells and Fireflies*. I recommend the latter especially: it's not a novel — just word pictures and portraits. I especially like Aunt Lena, whose double distinction it was that "she played the fiddle and was violently allergic to horse farts."

Painter Ken Tolmie, on the other hand, was born and raised elsewhere and came to live in Bridgetown for a time — deliberately, in order to be a rural painter, he says, at least partly because of his admiration for the work of "Peasant Bruegel" — and then left to become an urban painter in Toronto. You will probably want his book of portraits of Bridgetown people and scenes, entitled *A Rural Life*. You can see his paintings at The Gallery at Saratoga at Carleton Corner on Highway 201 on the southern edge of Bridgetown.

Both Buckler and Tolmie have a similar purpose: to look at rural life and see if *what it is* does not contain *what it is not*. Complex, eh? Which is to say that rural life is not simple in the least. Tolmie once said that a portrait of a farmer standing by his field was meant to catch the moment when the farmer changed the field and the field changed the man. Another painting (which has upset any number of viewers) has a hunter seemingly taking aim at his dog. Is the hunter about to shoot his companion? Tolmie is scornful of such easy responses. "Any rural person would see that the gun isn't cocked," he says. But what *is* being suggested?

My favourite Tolmie painting in *A Rural Life*, however, is of the little steer in the barnyard who is staring at the viewer. "When you put yourself in the picture," says Tolmie, "you're ankle-deep in mud and cowshit." He's deservedly proud of that. The rural life, he demonstrates, Ernest Buckler demonstrates, is not sufficiently depicted by "Old MacDonald Had a Farm."

You can ride through Buckler's words and Tolmie's pictures (and words, too — his text for *A Rural Life* is full of insights) on this loop out of Bridgetown. The ride is through beautiful farming country. Buckler and Tolmie ask you to think twice about beauty.

Where to Stay

There was a private campground right beside the bridge across the Annapolis River in Bridgetown, but when I was there it was closed and for sale. The alternative is to use the very beautiful and probably empty (there was not a single person in it when I visited) Valleyview Provincial Park atop North Mountain, 5 km (3 mi) north of Route 1 at Bridgetown. The view is spectacular. Open from mid-May through the first week in September. No mailing address available. *Valleyview Provincial Park; (902) 665-2559.*

The reason why the beautiful Valleyview Provincial Park will be empty is that it provides none of the services which most travellers desire — like electricity, flush toilets and hot showers. If you wish to cycle from the park you should be aware that the climb back up the mountain to the park will be a serious challenge and is not recommended for the recreational cyclist. It is probably a better idea to take your bicycle on your vehicle to the little town park with the big name, the Queen Elizabeth II Jubilee Park, in the centre of Bridgetown. Park your vehicle near the tourist information kiosk (where toilets are available) and cycle forth from there — which is what I did.

Cherryhill Bed and Breakfast, half a mile east of the Carleton Corner junction with Route 201, comes highly recommended by Ken Tolmie. There is in fact a portrait of its proprietor, Hilda FitzRandolph, in *A Rural Life.* She advertises a "full breakfast at the guests' convenience." *Cherryhill Bed and Breakfast, R.R. #4, Bridgetown, Nova Scotia B0S 1C0; (902) 665-4572.*

The Ride

This route is suitable for all kinds of bicycles, but I found the mountain bike especially useful riding the paved but narrow shoulder of Route 1.

Find Queen Elizabeth II Jubilee Park (with the tourist information kiosk) in the centre of Bridgetown, on Route 1, which is here called Granville Street West. The ride begins here.

Leave the park and turn right, easterly, through the centre of town (the T junction of Granville and Queen Streets) and take the first turning left, northerly, which is called Church Road, which is also known as the Hampton Road. Ride northerly on Church (Hampton)

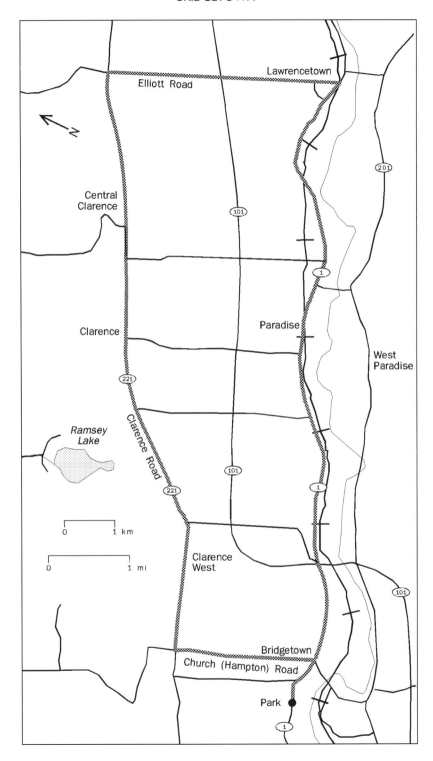

Road to the Clarence Road, which is the first road you meet. It is marked. Turn right, easterly, on the Clarence Road and ride until you come to the clearly marked Elliott Road. Turn right, south, and ride on the Elliott Road to Lawrencetown.

(At Lawrencetown you might be tempted to ride the old railbed back to Bridgetown. The use of this railbed is disputed here as elsewhere. But I tried it anyway, and found the railbed too soft — deep sand — even for my mountain bike.)

At Lawrencetown, turn right, westerly, on Route 1. The traffic is less than you might expect because in this locality the superhighway (Route 101) carries most of the traffic. Route 1 has in fact a good (but narrow) paved shoulder. (And Route 201, should you want to consider it — on the south side of the river — has no shoulder at all.) Nonetheless, I was glad I was riding a mountain bike because when two cars encountered one another beside me, I found myself bouncing along in the dirt beside the paved shoulder, and was pleased to do so.

So ride Route 1 from Lawrencetown back to Bridgetown. You will ride through Paradise (who could miss the opportunity?) and you will in fact see Paradise Station (imagine stepping off the train here on a cold and snowy night), which has, alas, fallen to ruin. Think theologically — once again.

ANNAPOLIS ROYAL

DISTANCE: 42 km (26 mi)	**OTHER FACTORS:** A long pull in
TIME: 2 hrs	granny-gears returning by
DIFFICULTY: Moderate to Difficult	Parker's Mountain.

Lillian Russell's Bicycle

There's something to be said for excess. Probably too much. But — this may surprise you — there is a history of excess hereabouts. For example, I am staying (as you might be) at Bread and Roses, an inn in Annapolis Royal much favoured by cyclists from nearly everywhere (the Annapolis Valley is a mecca for recreational cyclists), and Bread and Roses is an Edwardian household, and you know how the Edwardians felt about austerity. They were against it. They liked the word *opulent*. I do as well. Makes me think of a beautiful woman ten pounds overweight falling out of her lingerie. Makes me think of Lillie Langtry (King Edward's great good friend) and, more especially, of Lillian Russell, the flamboyant beauty from Clinton, Iowa, who bested Diamond Jim Brady in an eating contest by shucking her corsets. It's a legendary story. Did you know that she rode a diamond-studded bicycle? The great food writer, M.F.K. Fisher, says she did. After a nice ride Lillian and Diamond Jim tucked into five-hour feasts. Our kind of people, no? My kind of people, yes.

You will find it easy to think about her at Bread and Roses — a hostelry which takes its name from a poem celebrating some women garment workers on strike in the States near the turn of the century. They demanded just wages because they needed bread, they said. But they were also women — and they wanted roses, as well. I can see all sorts of contemporary figures frowning disapproval. I can see Lillian Russell applauding. I can see Lillian Russell with a slow and knowing look. I like it here.

But I like it out there, too, on the cool road in the early morning mist, cycling out to Port Royal Habitation. The distance is 14 km (9 mi) from Annapolis Royal to Port Royal Habitation, and the visit to Port Royal is a stop on the suggested loop. Port Royal Habitation is a contemporary reconstruction of an early seventeenth century French fortified trading post. Would you believe that there is excess here as well? There was.

Cast your mind back. It is 1604-5. In London, *Othello* is playing before the court; white handkerchiefs are all the rage. Francis Bacon has published *Advancement of Learning*, and the scientific spirit is upon us with a vengeance. It will lead to earnest TV doctors selling us what they say is good for us. In Spain, Miguel de Cervantes produces the first part of *Don Quixote*, and all Europe falls over itself laughing.

Meanwhile, an intrepid band of French adventurers, traders and priests has ventured into outer space and fetched up on the shores of the Annapolis Basin where, under the leadership of Samuel de Champlain and Sieur de Monts, they found Port Royal Habitation. To the Natives who provided the furs, the Frenchmen must have looked like men from Mars.

Furs were big business back then. There was money to be made in the luxury trade. Trade was brisk.

There were of course the usual problems of living in an outpost on the edge of the known world. (That is their point of view you understand; the Natives had a different perspective.) But for the French, life can be tedious and exhausting: all that watching of the forest which stretches beyond knowledge; nothing and nothing but trees and shadows. All of that watching of *forever* can wear a fellow out. What could you measure the forest against? There was no end to it, and no maps. And remember that this was a gender-specific adventure. Good fellows all, we're sure, and sincere priests, but no representative of the charming other gender which was left behind in France.

Something had to be done. Theatre would have to do. Marc Lescarbot, the resident playwright, whipped up a production of *The Theatre of Neptune* to present to Samuel de Champlain when the commander returned from explorations round the Bay of Fundy. It was apparently well received.

But it was Champlain himself, ever mindful of the troops' morale, who founded the "Order of Good Times," a drinking and dining club which met in the assembly rooms of the Habitation (you can imagine the feasts). The Order inspired successors everywhere — from the gentry's clubs in London to "Cheers" in Boston — and heaven knows how many beer commercials. The "Order of Good Times" kept the fellows reasonably happy. A good pig-out is a traditional substitute for rarer sensual pleasures, and the measure of success is a good deal too much. You can forget (for a while) about being lonely when stupefaction is exultation.

And, as you will see when you visit the Habitation, the fortified trading post is in many ways a boy's delight. A cunningly designed square with a courtyard in the centre, it has guns which defend all approaches. It feels quite safe. You think you can play soldiers here for a long time. It is very attractive. You want to get right down on the carpet and play.

But the seventeenth century competition, a group of Brits down in Virginia, did not like sharing the continent with the French. It didn't matter that nobody knew how big the continent was. To know the other guy was somewhere was bother enough. (The Natives were neither consulted nor considered.) In 1613 the Brits came up from Virginia and burnt the place to the ground.

Where to Stay

As usual in Nova Scotia, the campgrounds are iffy hereabouts, and I saw none worth visiting, never mind considering. But if you are on a budget you might want to think about Tom's Pizzeria and Helen's Cabins on Route 201 east, just off the junction with Route 8. The cabins looked a good clean substitute for camping, and the pizza (I can speak for the pizza) was very good. Open from the middle of May through the middle of October. *Helen's Cabins, R.R. #1, Annapolis Royal, Nova Scotia B0S 1A0; (902) 532-5207.*

Would Lillian Russell have eaten pizza? You bet she would! A piece in each hand and a sleepy smile.

Bread and Roses Country Inn accommodates some of the international cycling tours, so you know cyclists are welcome. It is a restored Victorian mansion stuffed with antiques. In the evening there is tea, and the evening I was there, there was much talk, and the talk was superior. *Bread and Roses Country Inn, 82 Victoria Street, Box 177, Annapolis Royal, Nova Scotia B0S 1A0; (902) 532-5727.*

The Ride

You will want a mountain bike for this ride, or a hybrid. There is a stretch of dirt road.

Leave Annapolis Royal in an easterly direction on Route 1 and cross the bridge and make the hairpin turn in a westerly direction through Granville Ferry toward Port Royal. Follow the signs for Port Royal. It is 14 km (9 mi) from Annapolis Royal to Port Royal. Enjoy a feast of the imagination at Port Royal Habitation (you will find bilingual guides in period dress), and then retreat back down the road on which you came for a distance of some 100 metres, where you will see a sign indicating Hollow Mountain Road. Hollow Mountain Road leads uphill to your left; it is dirt. Turn left on Hollow Mountain

Road and begin the gentle climb up what is known as North Mountain, here at its most benign. Trust me; it's tougher elsewhere. When you are at the crest you will gaze out upon the Bay of Fundy, and then you will zip down to Delaps Cove. Here you will meet a paved road. Turn right (easterly) and ride to Parkers Cove, where you will see a working fishing wharf. About 2 km (1 mi) further along the paved road, turn right on Parker's Mountain Road. You will need your granny-gears. You may well have to stop to catch your breath at the top, and take the opportunity to damn me. Why did I bring you this way? For the view, of course. And then, when you begin your zinging descent (remember to *brake all the way down*), you may notice that this side of the mountain is even steeper than the other side, and *voila!*, you understand why you are riding in this direction instead of the other. At the bottom of the hill you intersect with Route 1 at the ubiquitous Irving station. Turn right (west) and ride on Route 1 — you have something of a paved shoulder — back to Annapolis Royal.

Another Ride

You may glance at the map and think that it might be a pleasant ride to leave Annapolis Royal on Route 201 and ride to Bridgetown on that road, cross the Annapolis River at Bridgetown, and return to Annapolis Royal on the other side of the river on Route 1. I thought so as well. But Route 201 is narrow and heavily travelled by cars and trucks and it has no shoulder at all. I think it is too dangerous for fun. Route 1, ironically, although even more heavily travelled than Route 201, has the advantage of something of a paved shoulder. Think long and hard and twice before you take this ride. It is 50 km (31 mi), 2 hrs 30 min.

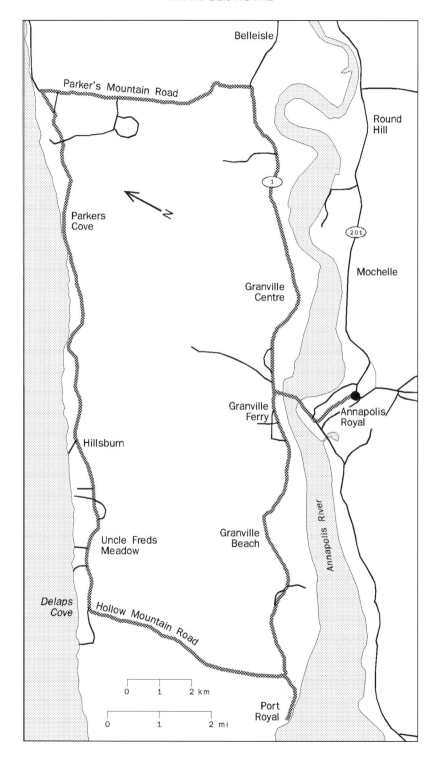

Belleisle

Parker's Mountain Road

Round Hill

Parkers Cove

N

1

201

Mochelle

Granville Centre

Granville Ferry

Annapolis Royal

Hillsburn

Granville Beach

Annapolis River

Uncle Freds Meadow

Delaps Cove

Hollow Mountain Road

0   1   2 km

0   1   2 mi

Port Royal

LUNENBURG

DISTANCE: 32 km (20 miles)	**OTHER FACTORS:** Wind off the
TIME: 1 hr 30 min	Atlantic.
DIFFICULTY: Easy to Moderate	

Looking at Houses

I digress:

Once upon a time, in a faraway city, I was perusing a book which I had picked from a display shelf in a book shop, when the postman — who was delivering mail to the bookstore — paused beside me. "That's a good book," he said, nodding to the volume I had in my hand, "you'll like that book." After that recommendation, what could I do but buy it? I did.

And he was right. I did like that book, and recommend it most heartily to you now, just as you are preparing to ride through and out of the old seaport town of Lunenburg. The book is Witold Rybczynski's *Home: A Short History of an Idea*. Rybczynski, born of Polish parentage in Edinburgh, Scotland, and educated in Britain and Canada, is now a practicing architect in Montreal and professor of architecture at McGill University. He wrote the book because he discovered that his students had little notion of the history of the House, which — as a truly wretched poet once noted — must inevitably become a Home. It is a cheerful and light-hearted book, and wickedly perceptive. Rybczynski notes, for example, that furnishing follows fashion, and that right now we are much influenced by designers such as Ralph Lauren, who began by designing clothes and then branched out into designing the furniture of our lives, and who is much influenced by movies. So it is not surprising (when you stop to think about it) that Rybczyski should perceive that, for a whole lot of us, a house is a theatre in which we play out our lives — or the notion of our lives which we wish to proclaim.

I should have noticed this a long time ago, I suppose, when my parents dragged me along to Open Houses and I followed them (scuffling my feet) through the rooms of the House in Question while they imagined how they might live in this particular building. And we all do much the same thing as they, don't we? "We'll put the boys in that room, and Wanda can have the little sunny place for her plants." And so on and on — and frequently we have no intention of buying a house at all. We are simply enjoying cheap entertainment.

If you are very lucky you might find an Open House at one of the older homes in Lunenburg, and thereby imagine yourself part of the family of a merchant of the nineteenth century who made perhaps a small fortune out of fish or shipbuilding. Or you might at least be able to sneak a look in a window. You will likely find that these are rooms big enough to accommodate large gestures: you can make a point at full stretch in one of these rooms. And a piano seems suitable here. Yes, there should be someone caressing a tune from the piano while you think long and sprawling thoughts. Your beautiful daughters can dance.

At the very least you will want to idle about the town, considering its business and imagining yourself in this dwelling, or that one, and pondering life in a town facing the sea, and perhaps remark to yourself or your companion how cozy a town seems which was built for people who lived in large houses close to one another (the freedom of space was inside, not outside), and who were accustomed to walking down to the harbour, to work, to the shops, and trudging back up again.

Inevitably you will contrast Lunenburg with your average suburb, with its fake estate in the lawn up front, and the tyranny of the automobile. The true master of the suburb is the car in the driveway; the house is attached to the garage to serve it. You can spend your life caring for the damned beast.

It is the houses out on the bicycle ride, however, which interest me most. You'll see them along the LaHave River: sturdy graceful houses of stacked horizontal lines and verticals, and roof-pitches that take rain, sleet, snow and sun — and throw the light back into the distance, over the shimmering water, across the river. These are houses which take account of the landscape and the water and the wind — and assert human dignity here. It is worth the trip to look at these houses. Their builders were people with a marvellous understanding of proportion: of house to landscape, of human to house. The comforting proportions are yours for the looking.

Where to Stay

Lunenburg offers unusually welcoming accommodation. There are several superior inns, and an excellent campground operated by the Lunenburg Board of Trade.

The Lunenburg Board of Trade Campground is in the centre of

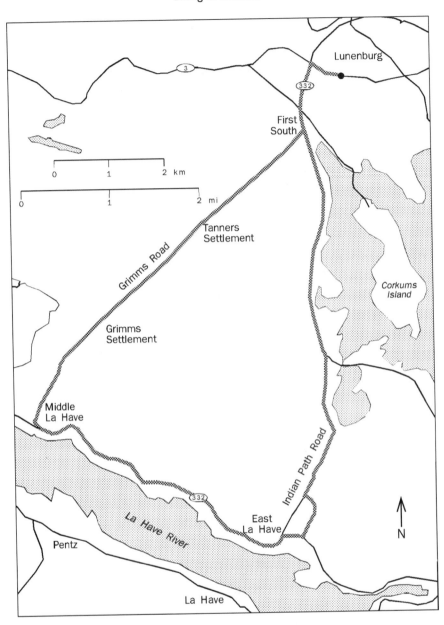

town, right next to the tourist information centre on Blockhouse Hill Road. There are flush toilets and free hot showers and a good view. The campground is open from May 15 through October 10. *Lunenburg Board of Trade Campground, Box 1300, Lunenburg, Nova Scotia B0J 2C0; (902) 634-8100.*

And among the superior accommodations available in Lunenburg, there is one which is ideal for cyclists: the Blue Rocks Road Bed and Breakfast — and Bicycle Barn. Yep, Merrill Huebach runs the very comfortable and quietly elegant bed and breakfast (do you fancy scrambled eggs — with salmon bits—for breakfast?) and Al Huebach (who has ridden bicycles very long distances as well as up and down very steep hills with reckless abandon) runs the Bicycle Barn, where repairs and rental bicycles are of course available, and gear is for sale — and new bicycles, of course, of a superior sort. As you might imagine, the talk at such an establishment is quite wonderful and is sometimes about bicycles; and Merrill knows exactly what carbohydrates cyclists require to maintain their verve uphill and down, and then she adds little touches like fresh strawberries and thick chocolate chip cookies. Advice on where to ride is of course readily given. *Blue Rocks Road Bed and Breakfast, R.R. #1, Garden Lots, Lunenburg, Nova Scotia B0J 2C0; (902) 634-3426.*

The Ride

If you are comparatively new to cycling, this is a good route for you. It is one of Al Huebach's lazy afternoon rides. All of the roads are paved, so you can use a ten-speed if you have one.

Make your way to the centre of Lunenburg, and ride out of town on Route 3 west until you meet Route 332, where you turn left (south). Follow Route 332 to the interestingly named community of First South, and there take the interestingly named Grimms Road on a pleasant ride southwesterly until you come to the LaHave River. You'll recognize it. At the river turn left (southeasterly) and ride alongside the river admiring the houses and water until you come to Indian Path Road. Turn left (northeasterly) on Indian Path Road and ride back to First South, where you meet Route 332 again and follow it to Route 3. Turn right (east) on Route 3 and ride back into Lunenburg.

GUYSBOROUGH

DISTANCE: 32 km (20 mi) from Guysborough, 27 km (17 mi) from Boylston Park **TIME:** 1 hr 30 min	**DIFFICULTY:** Easy **OTHER FACTORS:** Route 16 has no shoulders and the traffic is sometimes heavy.

Serenity

The ride here is very pleasant. It is not especially long, and not difficult at all. The scenery is quiet. You follow the route which is known locally as "doin' the tides." That is, you cycle out of Guysborough to the sign which directs you to Roman Valley. It is worth the trip to cycle towards those words. Imagine the people who settled here and chose that name. Consider the classical past and the example set by the Roman Empire for our lives and what that example demanded: duty, plainness, simplicity. Imagine Cincinnatus leaving his plow in the field to go save Rome from the barbarians in the fifth century B.C. Oh, all right, if you insist, you can think of Roman baths and voluptuous behaviour and dying gladiators, roaring lions, screaming crowds in the coliseum and politics by poison.

You are cycling, however, along the waters of the Milford Haven River. It is quiet. Better to think of duty, plainness, the virtue of water, virtue clear as water. On the dirt road which crosses the marsh, at the point where the water gathers into a channel, I saw a blue heron and an ambling porcupine. Then I rode back along the other side of the water until I saw the river give itself to the tranquil bay and thought I had found serenity. Serenity is exemplified by gently flowing water. Not a bad emotion.

Back in Guysborough I found myself in a Theatre of Past Hopes. You can see it in the grand Victorian red stone federal building which is the centre of the community. It is prominently dated 1903. Serious commercial activity was expected. But expectations went awry in 1903; the community became something smaller and other than what was assumed — or dreamed.

Is that bad? It is quiet here.

But there is another theatre in Guysborough: the Mulgrave Road Co-op Theatre Company is a group of actors committed to social responsibility. They have their offices and rehearsal space in an old building on the main drag. They want to entertain, of course, but they also want to invoke understanding in their audiences.

They travel a lot. The company typically visits a community and then creates a play for that community out of the people they meet there. Then they portray on stage characters — by name — who are looking at them from the audience. I call that daring and courageous and admirable.

But the idea is to provide a mirror of questions for the community in which the community can at once recognize itself and its problems and perhaps work for a solution. How does one respond to a strike in a one-industry town, for example? That sort of thing. Lively, innovative theatre. Not your usual sort of bubble-gum theatre which pops and is gone from mind and interest as you walk out the door.

They often perform here in the Guysborough masonic hall. Go see them perform.

Where to Stay

There is a private campground at Guysborough which advertises all the necessities for a cyclist, and more, but I do *not* recommend it. I have stayed there. In the words of a legendary French ambassador to Somewhere or Other, I shall have to seek another occasion on which to manifest my esteem.

If you are camping you would be wise to use the Boylston Provincial Park on Route 16, where I have also stayed. You will find it beautifully groomed and probably empty. Reservations are not accepted, but you will not need reservations. There will be *NO* electricity, showers or flush toilets. The grounds will be beautifully quiet; you will re-acquaint yourself with the old smell of human. Think about Roman virtue. No address is available. *Boylston Provincial Park, Boylston, Nova Scotia; (902) 533-3326.*

On the main drag (Route 16) in Guysborough you will find Grants Hotel Bed and Breakfast, venerably furnished and open all year round. It offers 9 units: 3 with private baths; 2 with shared baths. Breakfast is the continental version; the dining room offers home-cooked meals. You will often find actors living here. *Grants Hotel Bed and Breakfast, Box 136, Guysborough, Nova Scotia B0H 1N0; (902) 533-3395.*

The Ride

You will want a mountain bike or a hybrid for this route, if only for the stretch of dirt road at the gathering of the waters of the Milford Haven River.

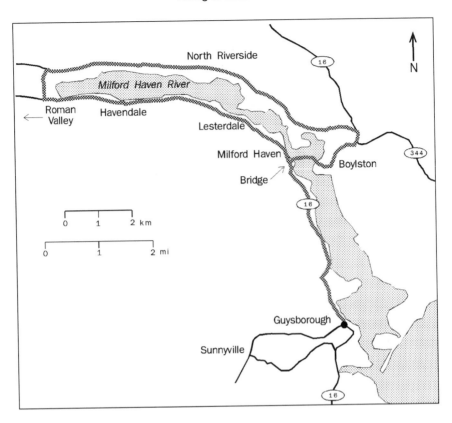

Cycle out of Guysborough in a northerly direction on Route 16 for about 6 km (4 mi) to the sign near the bridge which directs you to Roman Valley. Turn left, westerly, toward Roman Valley. The Milford Haven River is on your right. Take the first turn possible to your right. It is a dirt road which crosses the marsh where the water becomes a river. On the other side of the water you will turn right again and ride in an easterly direction along the northern bank of the Milford Haven. The road will be gravel for about 4 km (2.5 mi) and then pavement again as you approach and enter the pleasant little community of Boylston. You return to Guysborough on Route 16.

ISLE MADAME, CAPE BRETON

DISTANCE: First loop: Arichat/ Rocky Bay/ D'Escousse/Arichat, 25 km (15 mi). Second loop: Arichat/Petit-de-Grat/Little Anse/Arichat, 15 km (9mi)	**TIME:** First loop: 1 hr 15 min Second loop: 1 hr **DIFFICULTY:** Easy to Moderate **OTHER FACTORS:** There are a couple of granny-gear hills.

Disquisition on the Picturesque

All art is reductionist.

How's that for a thought to take on a bicycle ride?

It's true, anyway. When you paint a picture or take a photograph (or write a poem, story, novel), you have either transformed the experience into a work of art (which has its own value in itself, and for which the subject matter is merely the opportunity), or you have reduced the experience to a reminder of it.

But reminders are good. You do have a camera with you, don't you?

You will probably want to photograph the waves breaking over the rocks and the spray flung sparkling into the blue sky. That sort of thing. You walked away with some salt spray on your face.

Or the great view past the village to the sea. The village is a collection of colours, dots really, against the vast grey sea which seems to represent eternity. What are humans but blips?

But, quite often, when you get your photographs developed you have the feeling that you have somehow been cheated. You might immediately buy grander photographic equipment (I know people who have done this), or you might begin to rethink what you've done. You have reduced your experience to a reminder of it. That's OK. You can remember the spray on your face. But don't expect your friends to understand you.

"It was great," you might exclaim, showing your friends your photographs.

"Uh-huh," say your friends, looking around. You'd better give them some fresh drinks, quick.

But worse things can happen. Say you go off to experience the sublime view (waves on rocks) but make the error of driving your car there. I know, I know, *you* won't; *you* have a bicycle. But thousands will. They will drive to the advertised scenic view and get out of their automobiles and mill about looking at the scene ("beautiful, just beautiful," they murmur) and click away with their cameras before crawling back into their cars and driving home with their photographs which are so much litter. They have cheated. We know that, don't we? But they have cheated only themselves.

There is still worse. Hard to imagine, but yes. We mustn't flinch from this. One can be trapped into looking at the *picturesque*, which is a scene already arranged for reproduction on a postcard. The town council has put out flowerpots. There is a tea room or coffee shoppe designated *Ye*. There is no longer even the experience of looking at something; what you are visiting is somebody else's photograph.

There is only one thing worse than the picturesque — and you don't really want to think about it, do you? All right: it's the theme park. The theme park is one of the major embarrassments of our time. The theme park is dedicated to the pursuit of the Cute. It doesn't bear thinking about.

No, the only way the Sublime — the overwhelming view — can be known is by experiencing it, and the experience requires participation, and therefore effort. The automobile won't do it for you. Come to think of it, neither will any kind of convenient conveyence. Wordsworth made a fool of himself when he took a carriage out to look at Tintern Abbey (you may recall the poem — oh, the joys of pastoral landscape!), but when he got serious about knowing the size and magnificence and terror of nature, he and his cronies went gnawing up the peaks of the Alps. Grunt is required. Good thing you brought your bicycle, isn't it?

At Rocky Bay you will see the reckless ocean playing on the rocks. Beyond Petit-de-Grat, at Little Anse, you'll see the community of colour balanced against the vast grey sea. You can take the experience back with you, but you can't give it to anyone else.

Isle Madame, by the way, is a fluently bilingual Acadian French fishing community where you can see fishing boats hard at work. The old courthouse in Arichat is an attractive architectural example, as is the Roman Catholic church, built in 1838. (St. Francis Xavier University was founded here in 1853 but moved to Antigonish in 1855.)

Where to Stay

The old-fashioned, privately operated Acadian Campsite on Route 320, 2.5 km (1.5 mi) east of Arichat was just fine for Joe Spartan. It has all the requisites (hot showers, flush toilets) as well as some

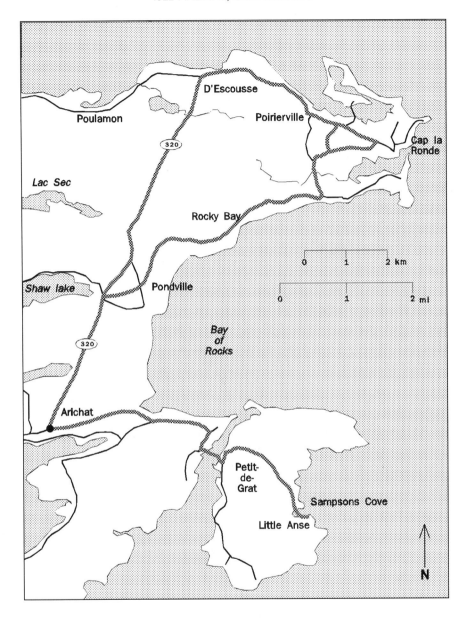

shade and a canteen. It is open from May 15 through October 15. *Acadian Campsite, Box 24, Arichat, Nova Scotia B0E 1A0; (902) 226-2447.*

L'Auberge Acadienne, on the main road (Route 320) in Arichat, is a big modern three-star inn decorated in the fashions of the last century. It is open the year round. Joe Spartan can only speak for the lunch he had here (it was very good) and the friendliness of the establishment, which was great and lively. Laughter is something which cannot be advertised, but (in my experience anyway) it is a good guide to a good place to stay. And the staff here can and will happily give you information about the island, including alternative cycling routes to the one I describe. *L'Auberge Acadienne, High Road, Box 59, Arichat, Nova Scotia B0W 1A0; (902) 226-2200.*

The Ride

This route is something of a figure-8, entirely on paved roads, and is consequently suitable for all kinds of bicycles. It can be easily shortened if you so desire.

Ride north from Arichat on Route 320 to Rocky Bay Road. Look carefully for the signs. One road turning off to your right is South Pondville Road, which is a pleasant scenic diversion, but not part of this ride. Another road turning off to the right is the North Pondville Road, which leads to the provincial picnic park and beach, which is also excellent, but not part of this ride. You want the scenic Fleur-de-Lis route, which is Rocky Bay Road. Turn right on Rocky Bay Road and ride northeast along the coast experiencing the sublime seascapes. Whales and seals are said to be seen but (of course) I saw none. At the next T there is a road marked No Exit leading to Cap la Ronde, which might be yet another fine scenic diversion, but I ignored the opportunity. Then, looking over my shoulder, I noticed that this end of Rocky Bay road is termed the Bono Road. That is, the same road seems to have two different names, depending on which direction you are travelling. By whatever name, I was at a T, and I turned left, westerly, through a community termed Poirierville to D'Escousse, where I met Route 320. I turned left (south) on route 320 and rode back to Arichat.

I continued through Arichat and turned left on the road to Petit-de-Grat. You will cross a bridge. I cycled out to the view at Little Anse, and then returned on the same road to Arichat — another approximately 15 km (9 mi).

MABOU, CAPE BRETON

Ride One
Mabou - Port Hood - Mabou
DISTANCE: 31 km (19 mi)
TIME: 1 hr 30 min
DIFFICULTY: Moderate
OTHER FACTORS: Gravel road

Ride Two
Mabou - Mabou Mines - Mabou
DISTANCE: 24 km (15 mi) to
Duncreigan Inn (Mabou Bridge);
37 km (23 mi) to Ceilidh Cottages
on West Mabou Road.
TIME: 1 hr to Duncreigan Inn,
2 hrs to Ceilidh Cottages
DIFFICULTY: Moderate to Difficult
OTHER FACTORS: Creature

Ride Three
Mabou - West Lake Ainslie -
Mabou
DISTANCE: 45 km (28 mi)
TIME: 2 hrs 30 min (4 hrs if you
use the rail-line from Lake
Ainslie to Glendyer.)
DIFFICULTY: Moderate;
Difficult if you use the rail-line.
OTHER FACTORS: The use of
the old rail-line between West
Lake Ainslie and Glendyer is
only for skilled, experienced,
fit cyclists.

The Most Sophisticated Place in Canada

I came to Mabou initially because I wanted to see where my best friend, Ray Smith, grew up. Ray Smith is the author of *Cape Breton is the Thought Control Centre of Canada, Lord Nelson Tavern, Century,* and *A Night at the Opera.* They are very fine books of fiction, which I have persistently and consistently misunderstood, and have always been forgiven for it. The first is a collection of stories; the last three are novels. I play a role in *Century* and have enjoyed it hugely. Smith has given me fantasies to perform which I had not yet got around to imagining. I am pleased and grateful for the opportunities. To hang around in somebody else's book is a delight.

Smith is himself a very sophisticated fellow who once said out loud, in public, on the radio, for everyone to hear, "Cape Breton is the most sophisticated place in Canada." It is not an opinion widely held (if even considered), but after a visit to Mabou you will understand what he means and quite possibly agree with him.

Mabou is a tiny community of distinctive vitality and culture. For one thing, it is perhaps the last place in North America where Gaelic was commonly spoken, and although you will not hear it on the road in Mabou today, children study the language in school to Grade Six, and the sign over the post office in the centre of Mabou is in Gaelic: *TIGH LITRICHEAN.*

But that post office has further significance, as well. You will see some indication of it on the large sign which greets you as you cross the bridge into Mabou. The sign features a picture of a mailbox and a depiction of a Canadian flag and these words:

WE SHALL FIGHT IN THE STREETS AND RURAL ROUTES
WE SHALL FIGHT ON THE FARMS AND ON THE WHARVES
WE SHALL FIGHT IN MABOU AND IN OTTAWA
WE SHALL NEVER SURRENDER

Why the anger? Because the bureaucrats of Canada Post in Ottawa deemed Mabou no longer worthy of a post office, that's why. The villagers protested and won — after a fashion. The post office still functions as it once did, and in the same building, but now it must be a business, and is. Mabou has adapted to the enemy and survived.

And flourished — in many ways. Mabou is famous across Canada for its music. The Rankin Family singers hail from here, and John Allan Cameron, and the Mabou fiddlers are renowned. Every Canada Day (July 1) a Scottish picnic and Ceilidh are held in Mabou. A Ceilidh (pronounced kay-lee) is a Scottish celebration which features Scottish country dancing. The country dancing may be step-dancing, or it may be graceful patterns, or it may be akin to something like joyful unarmed combat, but it is always taken seriously. (It was once required — and may still be — that a young officer in a Scottish regiment in the British army must demonstrate his skills as a dancer before he can be accepted in the mess.) And it was in Mabou where I came across one of my favourite images of the Maritimes: a small boy with his violin case waiting outside the doorway of the Bridge Museum for his music lesson. From inside came the sounds of another earnest learner. You're not likely to see that picture anyplace else.

No, what is important about Mabou is that history, art and skill are taken seriously. Smith is right. It is a very sophisticated place.

And its sophistication has been recognized and carried on in a quite surprising way by the *avant-garde* Mabou Mines theatre troupe. Oh, don't look for them up the road in Mabou Mines. You will have to go to New York City to see them at their home base, although you might well find them at the more sophisticated theatre fringe festivals around the world. How did they come to call themselves *Mabou*

Mines? Because once upon a time a member of the troupe was from this section of Cape Breton, and he gave the company access to a nearby children's camp where they met one summer to rehearse and create. They wanted a name for their company which was at once euphonious and did *not* suggest anything theatrical. They hit upon *Mabou Mines*.

And what will you see if you cycle up to Mabou Mines? You will see the sea from the promontory heights. Mabou Mines was a thriving coal mining community at the turn of this century, but the mines went down from the cliff to burrow under the sea and the sea could not be kept out. The mines closed in 1914, and what was once a community of a thousand people is now a memory and a view.

Nothing much, in fact, to write about, unless it's the dog. I met him first when I drove my little Ford Mustang along the road to Mabou Mines on a preliminary trip to Mabou, long before cycling season. Halfway along the gravel road which leads to the old mining site, I came upon the dog standing in the middle of the road. A woman — presumably the dog's owner — was nearby.

I am a courteous, humane fellow (honest!), so of course I slowed to a halt. Didn't want to hit the pooch. He held his ground. She called him. He ignored her. He held his ground. I smiled at her and gave a vague, if cheery, gesture with my hand. Life is full of little problems, eh? She called the dog. He ignored her. He stood his ground. I beeped my horn. He attacked my tire. Funny, I thought. That dog is going to ruin his teeth. Steel-belted radials are going to play hell with his canines. Ho-ho.

I beeped, she came and dragged him away by his choke-chain. Did I mention he was barking like hell between bites? He was barking like hell between bites. His whole body was thrown into that barking. He was a determined, dedicated dog. I made a mental note to remember him.

But I didn't know the half of it. Seems he was only practising on me. Later he got good at it. And when I returned later to cycle in Mabou I was told that he had disabled *six* cars. Yep. You'd better believe it. *Six* cars. Bit right through the tires.

"G'wan," I said. "Never."

"Six cars" said the speaker. The speaker was David Mullendore, operator of the Mull Restaurant in downtown Mabou. "Bit right through the tires."

"G'wan," I said.

"And one of them was mine."

"G'wan," I said. "What's that dog's name?"

"That dog's name," said David Mullendore, "is Mud."

A short time later I dropped by the Bridge Museum in Mabou to chat with the young people there about cycling the roads hereabouts. They'll know things other people won't. "No," said the young fellow, "you don't want to use a ten-speed on the Colindale Road: blow your tires in a minute."

"What about the dog?"

"You mean the Crazy Dog of Mabou Mines Road?"

"The same. Name of Mud."

"That dog," said the young fellow, "That dog is crazy. My grandfather went visiting up there one day and when he came out he found the dog sitting on the roof of his car. That dog's crazy."

And well known, I thought. Before I left we talked about Gaelic in the community, and the young people said yes, they studied Gaelic in school up to Grade Six and yes, the young fellow said, his grandparents sometimes talked Gaelic at home. "How about you?" I asked. "How's your Gaelic?"

"Don't ask," he said.

So before I set out to ride my bicycle on the Mabou Mines Road I expressed my uneasiness (*uneasiness*, hell; I was scared) to a local friend who said not to worry — she would call the owner and have the Crazy Dog of Mabou Mines Road kept inside while I was riding by. Good, I thought. If that dog could disable *six* cars by biting throught their tires, what would he do with a bicycle? Eat the frame and use the spokes for toothpicks? And what of me, the rider? A line from Dylan Thomas swept unbidden into my head: "When their bones are picked clean and the clean bones gone." I was glad that dog was going to be kept inside.

And he was — he was kept inside a wire pen. As I heaved myself up the hill some twenty yards from him, I heard him flinging himself against the wire fence, using it as a trampoline: K-WHANG, K-WHANG, K-WHANG.

I made it up and back and it was a good ride and I want to thank publicly my friend who made the call and the person who penned the dog, and the good people of Mabou.

I hope that when I next return to Mabou — when you come to Mabou — that we shall again meet this dog. I hope to see this dog in the Bridge Museum. I hope to see this dog labelled MUD. I hope to see this dog Stuffed.

Where to Stay

As usual in Nova Scotia, camping can be a problem. There are two private campgrounds on Route 395 on the eastern side of Lake Ainslie, but they are a good 50 km (31 mi) from Mabou. There is another at Strathlorne on Route 19, which is 15 km (9 mi) from Mabou.

Much closer to Mabou are the Ceilidh Cottages, 4 km (2.5 mi) from Route 19 on the West Mabou Road. I stayed here on one visit. It is clean and tidy and has good hot showers and flush toilets and electrical hook-ups, and if you have a camper or a van or any sort of travelling home on wheels, it is quite excellent. I had my van. The establishment is open from June to October. There are in fact 10 housekeeping cottages available, and a swimming pool and tennis courts. There is only one catch: the proprietor refuses to accept tenters. Mean eh? *Ceilidh Cottages, P.O. Box 94, Mabou, Nova Scotia B0E 1X0; (902) 945-2486; (winter) (902) 945-2624.*

The Duncreigan Inn, just before the bridge at Mabou on Route 19, is a most superior country inn operated by Charles and Eleanor Mullendore, who have lived in exotic corners of the world and come to Mabou to offer you peace and quiet. It is a wonderful place to hide out from bother — preferably with someone you find congenial or possibly enchanting. There are good, interesting books and magazines in the lounge and lively conversation, which is always to be valued and difficult to find. The deck looks out upon Mabou Harbour, where once there would have been boats from the West Indies, but not any longer. Now the water is serene. There was once a little train station just up the way, but not any longer. It is quiet here now. Because this is a country inn (not a bed and breakfast; the distinction is important) the hearty and delicious breakfast costs extra, but the dining room also serves dinner, and you can dine very well indeed at your leisure after a good afternoon's ride and talk softly to your companion over glasses of wine. Moreover, bicycles are available! The season is April through 31 December (other times by arrangement). *Duncreigan Inn, Box 59, Mabou, Nova Scotia B0E 1X0; (902) 945-2207.*

Lunch is available at the only restaurant in town — which, luckily, is unusually good. It is operated by David Mullendore and is called the Mull, and you don't have to take my word for its quality. You may well have to stand in line, on a weekday, and the people in line are not even tourists.

The Rides
There are three rides out from Mabou, and one of them — along the sea to Port Hood — may well be the most beautiful ride in the world. But you'll have to go look for yourself, won't you?

Ride One
You will need a mountain bike for the gravel road.

The most beautiful ride in the world starts at the Duncreigan Inn. You can pick up the old rail-line just above the inn and ride in a southerly direction until you meet the West Mabou Road. Turn right (westerly) on the West Mabou Road (locally called the Colindale Road), and ride past the Ceilidh Cottages. The road will shortly turn to gravel; ride it along and above the sea and take in the uncluttered views until you meet pavement again just outside Port Hood. Turn left into Port Hood. There is a public beach with washrooms which you might want to visit in Port Hood. Continue through Port Hood until you meet Route 19. Turn left (north) on Route 19 and return to Mabou.

Ride Two
A mountain bike is required for this ride.

This ride takes you up the dirt and gravel road to Mabou Mines and back. I rode from the Ceilidh Cottages east to Route 19, and then along Route 19 into Mabou past the Duncreigan Inn and across the bridge. Just past the bridge will be a sign indicating Mabou Harbour Road. Turn left and ride down the hill and up the hill past the church and past the school and arena and onward into the country until you pass the road down to Mabou Harbour (ignore it for now), and shortly you will see the sign directing you to Mabou Mines off to your right. The road is gravel and is a pretty good climb uphill. At the top you will find yourself overlooking a valley which gives onto the sea, and, at the foot of a road off and downhill to your left, a little working harbour. This is Mabou Mines. The old mine shaft went down into the sea from the cliff above that little harbour. If you go close you will see signs warning you off; you would be wise (I think) to heed those signs. Return to Mabou and on to the Ceilidh Cottages the way you came.

Ride Three
This ride requires a mountain bike for the dirt roads beyond Brook Village.

I began this ride from the Duncreigan Inn. I crossed the road

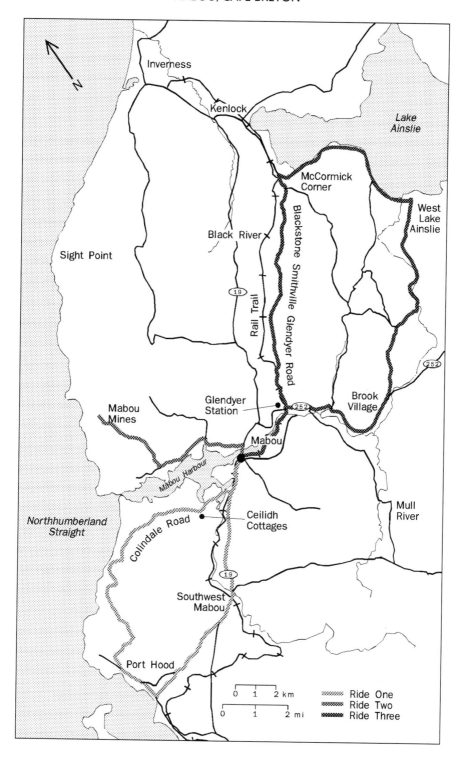

Inverness

Kenlock

Lake
Ainslie

McCormick
Corner

West
Lake
Ainslie

Black River

Blackstone Smithville Glendyer Road

Sight Point

19

Rail Trail

252

Mabou
Mines

Glendyer
Station

252

Brook
Village

Mabou

Northhumberland
Straight

Mabou Harbour

Colindale Road

Ceilidh
Cottages

Mull
River

19

Southwest
Mabou

Port Hood

0   1   2 km

0   1   2 mi

Ride One
Ride Two
Ride Three

(Route 19) just above the inn, and rode the old rail-line easterly behind Mabou to Route 252. The old rail-line (the Inverness & Richmond) has been converted to a path by the local snowmobilers — who need not be so particular about its surface as a cyclist might wish. It is good along here and elsewhere where the old coal-fired steam engines dumped their cinders.

Turn right (southeasterly) on Route 252 and ride the paved surface to Brook Village (about 10 km [6 mi]), where, at the Brook Village Grocery Store, you will turn left (northeasterly) on the dirt road and go straight, ignoring all other possibilities, to West Lake Ainslie. You are aiming for West Lake Ainslie Chapel. You will arrive at the Immaculate Conception Church and a T junction with a paved road. Turn left (northwesterly) on the paved road and ride on this road, ignoring all other possibilities, until you come to the sign directing you to Blackstone and Smithville. (It is just *before* the old rail-line.) Turn left (southwesterly) on this road, and look for the turning marked Glendyer. You will ride approximately 10 km (6 mi) (through Blackstone and Smithville, which you may not notice) to Glendyer, where you will meet Route 252 again. This is where you pick up the rail-trail for your return to Duncreigan Inn.

If you want a mountain bike challenge, if you enjoy solving dangerous problems of terrain very quickly, then you might want to consider using the old rail-line which parallels the Blackstone-Smithville-Glendyer Road. You pick up the rail line just beyond the turn-off for Blackstone-Smithville-Glendyer route described above and ride the rail-line on the return leg from Lake Ainslie to Glendyer, where you must give up on it and take the road to Glendyer Station. There was once a terrible train wreck here and you can see why. If you take the old rail-line you will have something over 10 km (6 mi) of challenges. I rode it — but I do not recommend it unless you want some difficult, demanding, skill-testing riding. There were sudden holes and washouts and fallen trees. I fell off my bike more than once. If you break a leg out here you won't be found until the snowmobilers come through next winter, if then. Scary. You should not ride this route alone, and, if you must, tell someone in Mabou where you have gone and when to expect you back and when to phone the Mounties.

Schwinn

It turns out that I was there at the beginning, although I didn't know it, of course. The beginning of the mountain bike, I mean. I was there before the founders of mountain biking—the fabled Gary Fisher, Joe Breeze, Tom Ritchey, etc. I am absolutely pre-historic, and not even from California, but I was hurtling down hillsides long before the reward was toking up at the bottom. But when tales are told of Repack Mountain — so named because you had to repack (with grease) your smoking coaster brakes (back-pedal brakes) at the bottom — I know whereof they speak. My father repacked mine.

I was eight. My father bought the Schwinn second-hand. Everything we had was second-hand, and not entirely because there was a war on. But at that time and that place (Waukegan, Illinois) a new bicycle was not to be had for any money, and one was lucky to have a bike at all. I was not only lucky; I was endowed with great good fortune. My father bought this big balloon-tired Schwinn from a neighbour whose son had been drafted into the Army. It had wide long-horn handlebars and a double-arced top tube. You can buy something similar now from L. L. Bean. I sometimes wonder if the orginal owner of this bike survived the war and if he did, if he asked anybody what happened to his big, beautiful bike. It had hardly been ridden at all.

I loved that bike. Not only did it have fat balloon tires and a wide, foam-rubber seat (we didn't use the term *saddle* — and foam-rubber was the predecessor of *gel*), but it also had a knee-action front fork. What was this? It was simple enough in concept: it was a big spring which stuck out obscenely just under the handlebars (some were vertical; mine was obscene) and took the shocks delivered to the front fork. The current versions have different brand names (like Rock Shox), but all sell for a fearful price. They have their benefits (downhill) and their drawbacks (uphill). I didn't notice either. I was too busy bombing through the ravines around Lake Michigan, hurtling over roots and rocks on my way from here to there, usually with a baseball glove hung over the handlebars by its strap. It was the way we lived.

And of course the Schwinn gave me the world — distant neighbourhoods and distant places where streets had been laid out in the hopes of the twenties and left bereft of dwellings in the Depression thirties. There were even military installations you could visit.

Once, late in the War, my father gave up school-teaching (which, generally, he loathed) for a time and we moved to Wisconsin. There, with other kids, I would ride out to the pea-fields, where German soldiers, still in their North African uniforms, were working under guard — a single U.S. soldier with a Thompson submachine gun. You can imagine how wonderful that machine gun was, especially to me. The German prisoners had the job of feeding the pea vines to this huge machine which broke down often. They certainly were not sabotaging it. They were delighted to be alive, in the sunlight, in Wisconsin, working among the stinking pea vines under the benign eye of a friendly guard (equally glad to be alive, on soft duty) while kids on bikes milled around and looked at them with amiable curiosity. To find Germans in North African uniform did not seem especially strange to us. Everything in the world was equally strange to us; we were kids. Everything in the world was equally usual to us; we were kids. So when the prisoners asked if they could ride our bikes around the area while the machine was being repaired, we were agreeable, and the guard didn't care. The prisoners were suitably romantic in their uniforms and different language. They took turns on my beautiful Schwinn, riding round and round, laughing with joy. I was pleased that they were so pleased. Later with the other kids I discussed the Germans' intriguing insignia.

So the bicycle gave me, gives you, the world and education. I could go where I liked so long as I was home for supper. Mother was particular about suppertime. And I had the requisite answer to the standard question

"Where have you been?"

"Riding around."

We simply absorbed the world with our wheels.

And of course, like you (I suspect), like most everyone who ever rode a bike as a kid, I had my head down dreaming one day and ran into the back of a parked car. I was flung over the handlebars and bounced off the car. No helmets in those days, of course. I could have been paralysed for life, but I wasn't. I picked myself up, got back on my bike, looked around to see if anyone had seen me do such a dumb thing, and continued on my way — as I still am.